Catholic Priesthood

FORMATION AND HUMAN DEVELOPMENT

Gerald D. Coleman, S.S.

Foreword by Thomas G. Plante, Ph.D.
Introduction by Katarina Schuth, O.S.F.

Liguori
LIGUORI, MISSOURI

D1279061

Published by Liguori Publications
Liguori, Missouri
www.liguori.org

Imprimi Potest: Thomas D. Picton, C.Ss.R.
Provincial, Denver Province, The Redemptorists

Imprimatur: Most Reverend Sylvester D. Ryan
Bishop of Monterey, California

Nihil Obstat: Msgr. Helmut Hefner
President and Rector of St. John's Seminary, Camarillo, California

Library of Congress Cataloging-in-Publication Data

Gerald D. Coleman.
    Catholic priesthood : formation and human development / Gerald D. Coleman ; foreword by Thomas G. Plante.—1st. ed.
        p. cm.
    Includes bibliographical references.
    ISBN 0-7648-1407-9 (alk. paper)
    1. Catholic Church—Clergy—Psychology. 2. Catholic Church—Clergy—Sexual behavior. I. Title.
BX1912.7.C65 2006
262'.14273—dc22   2006001173

The editor and publisher gratefully acknowledge permission to reprint/reproduce copyrighted works granted by the publishers/sources listed on pages 140-141.

Liguori Publications, a nonprofit corporation, is an apostolate of the Redemptorists. To learn more about the Redemptorists, visit *Redemptorists.com.*

Printed in the United States of America
10 09 08 07 06   5 4 3 2 1
First edition

This book is dedicated to past and current seminarians and faculty of St. Patrick's Seminary & University, Menlo Park, California, and to the priests of the Archdiocese of San Francisco.

With gratitude to the Carmelite Nuns, Carmel, California, and Samuel G. West.

Contents

Foreword

The Catholic priesthood in America has been experiencing highly tumultuous times of late. First, the number of young American men willing to become Catholic priests has been steadily declining over the past several decades at alarming rates. While there was about one priest for every eight hundred American Catholics in 1965, there is only about one priest for every fourteen hundred American Catholics today. Furthermore, the average age of an American Catholic priest is about sixty. Too few men are now willing to enter religious life, and many churches need to share priests with other parishes or even close their doors. Perhaps for many, a life of vowed chastity, obedience, and poverty is outdated and contrary to so many contemporary American cultural values and objectives. Second, the increasingly diverse American landscape has resulted in many more challenges for priests and parishioners alike. Priests and parishioners often come from different ethnic, cultural, and language traditions, which can create conflict and tensions. Many of the new seminarians and priests are foreign born with various cultural, ethnic, and language differences that need to somehow meld with the North American Church. Finally, and perhaps most importantly, the clergy sexual-abuse scandals in the American Catholic Church have kept all priests under the watchful microscope of the press, victim advocacy groups, lawyers, and the general population. Who would have thought that the words *pedophile* and *priest* would be so often associated with each other? It would be difficult to argue with the contention that the priesthood in America is currently in a state of crisis.[1]

For rank-and-file Catholics, as well as priests themselves, it can be a challenge to be optimistic about the future for priests in America and perhaps in other western countries. It is very easy to be discouraged. Many newspaper, magazine articles, television shows, and books have highlighted the challenging and highly stressful times for the priesthood. Books such as *Priests: A Calling in Crisis* by the well-known sociologist and priest, Father Andrew Greeley, talk of these remarkable challenges for the priesthood and the Church.[2] Many of these publications offer little realistic hope for the future state of the priesthood.

During the past decade and a half, I have evaluated over two hundred men who wished to enter religious life as a Catholic priest. Overall, as a psychologist and a Catholic, it has been inspiring to interview and evaluate these men of faith. The vast majority have been very committed to life in the priesthood, carefully evaluated the pros and cons of such a commitment, received appropriate consultation, and bring to the experience a remarkable list of gifts, talents, and experiences.[3] Relative to previous generations, these new applicants to the priesthood tend to be older, more mature, savvy, and have had educational and career experiences that are highly impressive. Some have been professionals, such as lawyers, doctors, engineers, teachers, mental-health professionals, among other careers. Some have been married and widowed. Some have experienced remarkable stressors as immigrants and refugees from war-torn or impoverished countries. So many of these men have had highly compelling alternatives to religious life and have agreed to sacrifice a much more comfortable life for their call to the priesthood.

Results from this study indicate that many modern-day applicants to the priesthood are well-adjusted individuals who are bright, socially responsible, emotionally stable, and interpersonally sensitive. Relative to a number of previous studies published several decades ago, the most current research suggests a more positive psychological profile of Catholic priest applicants.

Of course, not everyone who applies for vowed religious life is a good candidate. Some experience significant psychological and psychiatric vulnerabilities. Some desire the priesthood for selfish or unhealthy reasons. The evaluations conducted throughout seminaries in the United States seek to screen these individuals out, so that those who are troubled or at risk to themselves and/or others are encouraged to seek professional help.

Given all of the negative press attention priests and the priesthood have received in recent years, some of the newest generation of priestly candidates are inspiring. It is unfortunate that there are not many more.

Father Gerald Coleman's newest book, *Catholic Priesthood: Formation and Human Development*, is different than other contemporary books about the priesthood, and it is a welcome addition! His book is optimistic and inspiring. The first few chapters clearly articulate the call and response to the priesthood. His perspective accurately reflects the many men desiring to enter the priesthood.

Father Coleman then outlines many of the practical matters associated with human formation, sexuality, and celibacy. Finally, he focuses on problematic issues associated with formation, including the sexual-abuse crisis and related contemporary challenges to priestly formation. The work also contains several appendices that outline a code of ethics, how to take a sexual history, and warning signs of potential sexual abuse and sexual problems.

Throughout the book, the author maintains a practical and matter-of-fact tone that presents a positive and inspired view of the priesthood, both now and in the future. Father Coleman balances issues related to the significant challenges facing the priesthood with the inspired call to serve God and the Church in such a selfless and courageous manner. He also merges academic and theological scholarship with very practical, down-to-earth issues facing priests today. The book is especially useful for anyone—seminarians, teachers, priests, or laypeople—who has an interest in the future of the priesthood in the United States.

THOMAS G. PLANTE, PH.D.
PROFESSOR OF PSYCHOLOGY
SANTA CLARA UNIVERSITY
SANTA CLARA, CALIFORNIA
APRIL 15, 2005

Introduction

Over the past two decades Roman Catholics have focused increasing attention on those who serve as priests and on their preparation for this ministry. There is concern about the decreasing number of men who are entering the priesthood and, more recently, about their character and formation for service to the people of God. Recent sexual-abuse scandals have challenged the Church to reevaluate their primary modes of religious and ministerial formation. In the midst of these troubling times, the necessity of forming mature, holy men who can lead and unify the Christian community becomes all the more urgent. In light of the issues that challenge the modern Church, Father Gerald Coleman asks: "What kind of a priest do you want?" And further, "How can a formation program be designed to produce such a person?" Both questions are superbly addressed in this book. At a time of major transition in the Church, the answers will be key determinants of the future vitality of ministry. This book considers crucial aspects of human formation and development for those who are preparing to become priests and for those who already are serving.

Many have speculated about the structure and content of initial and ongoing formation of priests. The Scriptures are replete with references to qualities necessary for the presbyter who would lead the community. Theologians, ministers, and psychologists, among others, have clarified the primary biblical, theological, and psychological necessities of priestly formation. Especially since the publication of Pope John Paul II's *Pastores Dabo Vobis* in 1992, the fourfold foundation of formation—including human and spiritual, intellectual, and pastoral dimensions—is taken into account in many ministerial programs. The notion of "human formation" as a separate subcategory of priestly formation was essentially new in the formulation of John Paul II, and until the present book, its meaning has not been fully explored, described, or analyzed in one comprehensive work. In this volume, Father Coleman offers a rich and broad discussion of the complex issues related to the human formation and development of seminarians and priests.

Even before the current sexual-abuse problems, seminary educators were working to develop programs that would meet the formational needs of present-day candidates for the priesthood. Since the 1980s especially, it became obvious that many aspects of formation (for example, celibate chastity) needed to include more contemporary research as well as long-standing wisdom. With the diminishment of family life and growth in individualism in society, it has become apparent that even the basic understandings of community and friendship can no longer be taken for granted and, in fact, these core insights need to be stressed in the education of priests. Through the years, many have contributed to the body of literature and training programs that now constitute human formation for priests. Chapter by chapter, Father Coleman distills the best of what has been written about each area, and he augments these insights with his own years of study and experience as a seminary professor and rector. Interwoven in every chapter are carefully chosen biblical, poetic, literary, and historical references that illustrate the perennial interest in this topic.

In the first chapter of the book, the author considers the primary question of what it means to be a priest. The gospels identify the essence of the vocation: A priest is one who is called to follow after the pattern of Jesus' life. The call is demanding and lifelong, and it requires constant effort to overcome the inevitable weakness of the human condition. This work directs readers toward many documents and directives that specify how this call is to be developed in order to ensure that priests become whole and loving persons; including, for example, the appreciation of human sexuality and knowing the meaning of true friendship within a celibate context. Equally informative are references to contemporary and historical figures, whose witness gives life to the book's primary themes. For example, Father Coleman highlights Pope John Paul II's interpretation of the priest as shepherd: that is, one who empties oneself for the sake of service to others; or Karl Rahner, SJ, who emphasized the humanity of the priest—identifying with suffering and powerlessness, yet aware of God's grace at work in all circumstances; or, we can still learn from the sixteenth-century saint, John of the Cross, who spoke of three "enemies" of human formation—the world, the flesh, and the devil. Human formation, argues Father Coleman, begins with reflections on these and other diverse themes in a context characterized by trust in those who provide guidance for the journey toward priesthood.

Continuing the exploration, the second chapter deals concretely with virtues and qualities necessary for effective ministry; it also identifies human characteristics that inhibit such service. Based on "a special and profound rapport with Christ," the portrait of an effective priest emerges: one who possesses humility and authenticity, zeal and vision, one who is willing to labor tirelessly in the bond of communion with his bishop and fellow priests, and one who has the capacity for empathy, relationship, and dialogue. A person who embodies—or can develop—these characteristics has the potential for service as a priest, but one must also recognize other indicators that could threaten the priestly vocation. Regardless of one's empathy, humility, and collegiality, certain personality traits are known to obstruct—and sometimes destroy—otherwise healthy vocations, such as preoccupied, dismissive, and fearful individuals who may exhibit narcissism, restlessness, or widespread, distorted sexual preoccupation. For vocation directors who are helping men discern their suitability for priesthood, this chapter introduces important indicators of a call and describes the continual process of conversion required to reach a state of readiness to embark on the path that leads to ordination.

Having set forth the meaning and ideal of priesthood, the next chapter names the reality of what seminarians are actually like these days in terms of their human, religious, and intellectual profiles. In light of the tremendous diversity of background and potential, Father Coleman advises careful psychological assessment during the process of admission. Leaning on the work of Len Sperry's *Sex, Priestly*

Ministry, and the Church, the lists of psychological factors, requisite
ministry skills, capacities, experience, and negative predictors of vocational success serve as an imperative guide for those making decisions
about admission of candidates to priesthood. The author reviews other
psychological tests, the appropriate use of psychosexual history, and
assessment of human development—all of which contribute to effective screening. The goal of this process is not only to discourage admission of candidates who do not meet the requirements for priesthood
but also to make available useful data for formation directors as they
counsel those who are admitted to seminaries and religious communities.

Given the description of who can serve well as a priest and then
the conditions for admission of candidates who have the potential for
development and conversion, the next three chapters are central to
the purpose of the book. They are concerned with meaning: that is,
the meaning of human formation and development and the meaning
of human sexuality. The explanation of program guidelines provides
fresh insights into many aspects of formation. Drawing on major
church documents on the topic, as well as pertinent historical and
contemporary writings, these chapters cut to the core of formation
by suggesting that its task is "to be fully a human being" and "becoming good." Along the way the seminarian must work at being prudent
and discerning, becoming mature, free to take on the role of a public
person, and of solid moral character. Seminaries need to develop the
particular "markers of human formation" that will help the seminarian achieve these goals, not as hurdles to be overcome, but as the building blocks for lifelong growth as a priest.

Within this framework, issues of sexuality—always important—
have taken on added gravity because of the turmoil created by the
sexual-abuse crisis of 2002. The fifth chapter, in particular, addresses
the most critical concerns surrounding human sexuality and celibacy.
Signs of healthy affective sexuality include qualities of warmth, gentleness, and compassion, while isolation and a loveless existence signal
the opposite. Besides making careful distinctions about sexual orientation, sexual identity, intimacy, and asexuality, the author identifies

differences and sensitivities based on multicultural and multiethnic attitudes. Examples take into account various understandings of proper behavior toward women, family members, and communities, and they provide extensive information to assist in formational conferences and spiritual direction. The controversial topic of taking a sexual history is addressed thoroughly, as are ministerial and professional boundaries, friendship, and loneliness. The chapter is a gold mine of wisdom for formation personnel who might lack the vocabulary and courage to speak directly of these matters to their advisees.

The sixth chapter deals with problematic issues in human formation and development. These issues arise from "poor, inadequate, or nonappropriated" formation or perhaps insufficient screening in the first place. It covers sexual abuse of minors, violations against the sixth commandment, chronically wounded priests, and cybersex/internet addiction. Sadly, sexual abuse of minors has taken on immense significance since its frequency and seriousness have become well known. Especially since 2002, Church leaders have emphasized rules and norms as never before. It is incumbent upon all formation directors and all students to grasp fully the meaning of the definitions and the consequences of wrongful behaviors associated with sexual misconduct, and this section of the chapter is a valuable guide. The relationship of sexual abuse to violations against the sixth commandment deals helpfully with imputability and culpability; likewise responsibility for "chronically wounded priests" is considered in light of the canonical, biblical, and moral tradition. Finally, the author raises problems associated with cybersex/internet addiction, which ten years ago was a topic barely on the horizon; now it has become a matter of grave concern in society, including seminarians and priests. For each problem the author provides tools for reflection and evaluation that will prove indispensable for anyone concerned with human formation.

Since celibacy is regularly reinforced as a requirement for priesthood, the last chapter on celibacy as a lifestyle offers rich explanations in support of this discipline and way of life. Its witness value is drawn from biblical testimony and the Church's understanding of celibacy as a gift, a grace, and a charism. Personal appropriation of this gift is one of the main tasks of human formation, and it extends to spiritual formation as well. Coupled with celibacy, chastity authentically lived is the virtue that "makes it possible to create great intimacy with others." Since this intimacy does not include marriage and children, grieving these losses are important steps to full acceptance of the discipline. The chapter details the rationale for celibacy and the skills needed for celibate living that are to be embraced in a gradual process emerging from prayer and practice.

Although the issues and problems treated in this work can seem overwhelming, a thread of hopefulness runs throughout. Deep and abiding faith in the strength of God's grace is ever present. Several years ago in a survey of seminary rectors, they were asked to identify the most developed aspects of their programs related to formation for celibate chastity. They were also asked to mention unresolved issues and problems in dealing with formation for celibate chastity. In reviewing the vast array of issues on the list, it is fair to say that virtually every concern was addressed in this book. Underlying the attitude of hope for the future are two elements: knowledge and prayer. For those who are inclined to overly "spiritualize" sexuality, an awareness of the very real human condition of sinfulness we all share is clearly presented in this book. At the same time, the author is unambiguous about the fact that knowledge without an intense prayer life will not be adequate for those who are called to priesthood. The resources and reflections presented here will assist formation personnel, seminarians, and priests with the indispensable mission of holding both in balance.

SISTER KATARINA SCHUTH, O.S.F.
THE SAINT PAUL SEMINARY SCHOOL OF DIVINITY
UNIVERSITY OF ST. THOMAS
APRIL 14, 2005

1

The Call
"Come and See"

The work of priestly vocations is everyone's responsibility. The need for zealous and able priests in the United States is apparent, especially today, as the number of Catholics increase and the numbers of priests and seminarians decrease. This book is addressed primarily to seminarians (prospective or actual), priests, and those who form and direct them. Bishops, religious superiors, vocation directors, and faculty personnel all play critical roles in the formation process. However, such responsibility does not lie solely in their hands. Priestly formation belongs to the whole Church and its members. Therefore, this book is likewise directed to any believer: to you and me. If we accept the challenge to understand the human and spiritual dimensions of seminarians and priests, hopefully we will work and pray assiduously for priestly vocations.

One question centers our task: When a man receives a call to the priesthood, what does this mean for him and the Church? Since the awareness of the sexual-abuse crisis in the United States, a wide section of society—including bishops, vocation directors, seminarians, and priests—seek an understanding of this call, particularly its human dimensions. For the seminarian, clarity provides guidance; for the priest, it provokes self-examination; and for everyone else, it reveals the theological and pastoral framework of the priestly vocation.

In Mark's Gospel, after his baptism, Jesus announces that "the kingdom of God has come near." In this context, he calls his first disciples by the Sea of Galilee. Jesus "saw Simon and his brother Andrew casting a net into the sea....Jesus said to them, 'Follow me and I will make you fish for people.' Immediately they left their nets and followed him. As he went from there, he saw two other brothers, James son of Zebedee and his brother John, in the boat with their father Zebedee, mending their nets, and he called them. Immediately they left the boat and their father, and followed him" (see Mark 1:16–20 and Matthew 4:18–22).

Luke's Gospel situates this call by the Lake of Gennesaret. Jesus gets into Simon's boat and tells him to "put out into the deep water and let down your nets for a catch," and after catching "so many fish that their nets were beginning to break," the boats of Simon and his "partners" James and John "began to sink." This provoked Simon Peter to fall on his knees: "I am a sinful man." They brought their boats to shore, "left everything," and followed Jesus (see Luke 5:1–11).

The fourth gospel situates these callings in the setting of John the Baptist's announcement: "Here is the Lamb of God." Two of John's disciples heard this and followed Jesus who asked them, "What are you looking for?" They said, "Rabbi...where are you staying?" He said to them, "Come and see." They went and they stayed. These callings spread as Andrew told his brother Simon and brought him to Jesus, and the next day Jesus "found Philip." Philip, in turn, found Nathanael with the repeated invitation, "Come and see" (see John 1:35–51).

These biblical scenes give singular focus to the meaning of "come and see" for every disciple who desires to be with—and remain with—Jesus as a priest. The disciples are engrossed in their daily work and activities. Jesus sees them before they recognize him. The call is not self-initiated. When Jesus "saw" the ones he called, it was "not merely in the usual sense, but more significantly with his merciful understanding of men....'Follow me' means imitating the pattern of Jesus' life—not just walking with him."[1] The immediacy of their response denotes the depth of the call. [Their total abandonment of family indicates a profound sense of obligation] The specificity of the call (Matthew's Gospel indicates that there were others in the boats. See especially, verse 7) represents its deeply personal nature, and the mandate to "put out into deep water" shows its intensity, seriousness, and challenge. These calls were not vague. Despite their human failures and limitations, "They stayed with him that day" and forever.

Every authentic reply to the summons "come and see" must be situated in the context of the call of Jesus to his disciples. *The Basic Plan for the Ongoing Formation of Priests (BPOFP)*[2] complements the apostolic exhortation *I Will Give You Shepherds* (*Pastores Dabo Vobis*, or *PDV*) of Pope John Paul II and *The Directory for the Life and Ministry of Priests* from the Congregation for the Clergy.[3] These documents reinforce the point that priestly formation commences when the call is heard. Only then can a man enter a formation program and continue the call throughout his life and ministry. "Come and see" is not a one-time invitation. It is a guiding point-of-reference in every seminarian's and priest's life.

The fifth edition of the *Program of Priestly Formation*[4] follows the lead of Pope John Paul II's *Pastores Dabo Vobis*. Accordingly, priestly formation rests on four essential pillars: human, spiritual, intellectual, and pastoral.[5] All pillars are linked to form one single formational experience, and weakness in one area will doubtlessly create weakness in other areas. Formation must be aimed at total development in order to avoid imbalances: for example, overly intellectual formation limits human formation.

Pastores Dabo Vobis presents the starting point: "The whole work of priestly formation would be deprived of its necessary foundation if it lacked a suitable human formation….The priest, who is called to be a 'living image' of Jesus Christ, head and shepherd of the church, should seek to reflect in himself, as far as possible, the human perfection which shines forth in the incarnate Son of God and which is reflected with particular liveliness in his attitudes toward others as we see narrated in the Gospels. The ministry of the priest is, certainly, to proclaim the word, to celebrate the sacraments, to guide the Christian community in charity 'in the name and in the person of Christ….' In order that his ministry may be humanly as credible and acceptable as possible, it is important that the priest should mold his human personality in such a way that it becomes a bridge and not an obstacle for others in their meeting with Jesus Christ the redeemer of man."[6]

This image of *bridge* versus *obstacle* provides a benchmark for seminarians, priests, vocation directors, and formation faculty and personnel to measure the dimensions of human formation. If a seminarian or priest is a *bridge,* he must know the depths of the human heart, perceive difficulties and problems, and make meeting and dialogue easy. He creates trust and cooperation, expresses serene and objective judgments, loves the truth, and is respectful of every person. He is genuinely compassionate, a witness to integrity.

Pope John Paul II stressed the capacity to relate to others as especially important. "This is truly fundamental for a person who is called to be responsible for a community to be a 'man of communion.'"[7] A man of communion is not arrogant or quarrelsome, but affable, hospitable, sincere, prudent, generous, and ready to serve. He is capable of opening himself to true relationships, encouraging the same in others, and quick to understand, forgive, and console. He demonstrates affective maturity, possessing an authentic and comprehensive sense of love that involves his whole person. A viable education in human sexuality and true friendship is critical in order to learn and possess these levels of self-mastery that oppose all forms of selfishness. An education of the moral conscience lies at the heart of this transformation.

The *Directory for the Life and Ministry of Priests* affirms these same basic points. "As pastor of the community, the priest exists and lives for it; he prays, studies, works, and sacrifices himself for the community. He is disposed to give his life for it, loving it as Christ does, pouring out upon it all his love and consideration, lavishing it with all his strength and unlimited time in order to render it, in the image of the Church, Spouse of Christ...."[8] In *Pastores Gregis*, Pope John Paul II's 2001 Apostolic Constitution on Bishops, he counsels the same priestly posture, calling all priests and bishops to be "servants of hope" and "coherent pastors."[9]

Many years ago, almost presciently, Father Karl Rahner, SJ, captured this same perspective on human formation as communion:

The priest of tomorrow will be a man to whom mature people find their way even though society does not drive children to him. He will be a man who truly endures the grievous darkness of existence together with all his brothers and sisters, knowing that both its first source and its blessed fulfillment are found in the mystery of love which conquers by the incomprehensibility of the cross. Tomorrow's priest will be (otherwise he will not exist at all) a man able to listen, to whom every individual matters even though he be of no social or political importance; a man in whom one can confide, a man who practices the holy folly, or tries to, of bearing not only his own burden, but also the next man's; a man who, though he had the wherewithal and is no weakling, does not join in the desperate, neurotic pursuit of money, enjoyment, and other painkillers for the dreadful disappointment of existence, but, proves by his life that voluntary abnegation out of love of the Crucified, is possible and liberating. Tomorrow's priest will not have power drawn from the social power of the Church, but will have the courage to do without that power; he will believe that life comes out of death and that love, selflessness, the word of the cross, and the grace of God are strong enough to accomplish all that really matters in the end—causing man to give himself up willingly to the incomprehensibility of his existence in the faith and hope that God's incomprehensibility holds sway there as salvation and self-communicating.

Tomorrow's priest…will speak softly; he will not imagine that any eloquent argumentation of his can bathe in light the darkness of life and the constant assaults where he himself is defeated; he will still see God's grace at work where he himself can no longer present that grace with his word and sacrament in such a way that it is accepted precisely *through* them…; he will know that he himself is in God's service and on his mission….In a word, tomorrow's priest will be the man with the pierced heart, from whom alone he draws strength for his mission.[10]

With respect to his vocation, Thomas Merton recalled that he was deeply anxious when entering the cloister at Gethsemane, Kentucky. When first visiting this monastery for a Holy Week retreat, the porter asked him, "Do you intend to stay?" This question haunted him his whole life, and it remains an important mantra for every other seminarian and priest. "Come and see" provokes a deep and credible desire to stay, and it requires persistent attention. To answer the porter's question authentically, Merton recalled, he had to release his old self and experience a new self through constant conversion. "One of us has to die," he wrote.[11]

Human formation demands consistent self-reflection, coupled with a deep commitment to permit trusted others to assist and guide one's priestly journey and commitment. Priestly formation is meant to guide men into a greater awareness of their own gifts—strengths, weaknesses, opportunities, and threats. As shall be explored in the pages ahead, the most successful vocations emerge from those who are willing to empathize with people who see things differently, do not fall into rationalizations, know that there is something beyond self-interests, maximize personal efficiency, always strive to be objective, get the data before acting or reaching a decision, and are always prepared to reexamine one's reasoning. The call toward the priesthood, in other words, is a call to allow Christ to strengthen our human capacity to love with compassion, common sense, and conviction. One cannot change human nature, but one can nurture and develop qualities that bring Christ to life, thereby strengthening the conviction to answer "yes" every day to God's call.

Rise, Let Us Be on Our Way (Mark 14:42) contains Pope John Paul II's reflections on priestly vocations.[12] The pope's considerations serve as a worthy conclusion to this chapter, and bring us back to where we began. The mystery that roots every priestly vocation is found in Jesus' statement, "You did not choose me but I chose you…" (John 15:16). This call lies at the heart of every vocation. It enables one to carry out the remaining command, "…go and bear fruit that will last…." Every vocation is born in Christ. This fact alone gives dignity to every call. Enlightened by a sense of this personal call, a man must wholeheartedly devote himself to the "need of only one thing" (Luke 10:42). Holiness becomes the goal of every calling.

Since the earliest days of the Church, the image of the Good Shepherd has provided a model for ministry. The cover of the *Catechism of the Catholic Church* depicts a version of this symbol from a third century-Christian tombstone. According to Pope John Paul II, the figure suggests that "Christ, the Good Shepherd, leads and protects his faithful (the lamb) by his authority (the staff), draws them by the melodious sympathy of the truth (the panpipes), and makes them lie down in

the shade of the 'tree of life,' his redeeming Cross which opens paradise."[13] The "shepherd is for the sheep," says the pope, "not the sheep for the shepherd."[14] This image must be the leitmotif in every priestly life. Accordingly, John Paul II wrote, "I have decided to eliminate from my vocabulary the word 'my.' How can I use that word when I know that everything is Yours…? So I have learned that I may not say 'mine' of that which is Yours.…I must free myself, empty myself of this—I must possess nothing, I must not wish to possess anything."[15]

> I was ordained a priest at the age of twenty-six…Looking back, and remembering those [fifty-six] years of my life, I can assure you that it is worth dedicating yourselves to the cause of Christ, and for love of Him, dedicating yourselves to the service of others. It is worth giving your lives for the Gospel and for your brothers and sisters.[16]
>
> POPE JOHN PAUL II, MAY 3, 2003, MADRID

2

The Response
˝Becoming a Catholic Priest˝

Pastores Dabo Vobis opens chapter two with the scene of Jesus in the synagogue at Nazareth on the Sabbath (Luke 4:14–21). He reads from the scroll, indicating the fulfillment of Isaiah's prophecy by his ministry. Anointed with the Spirit, Jesus has come to preach good news to the poor, proclaim release to captives, give sight to the blind, to set at liberty those who are oppressed, and to proclaim the acceptable year of the Lord. Captivated by his pronouncement, "[T]he eyes of all in the synagogue were fixed on him" (Luke 4:20).

The eyes of the faithful are forever fixed on Jesus. As the priest proclaims the Good News, all eyes are likewise intently focused on him. The priest asks, "What do they see?" Do the faithful, in fact, see Christ? In order to maintain the authenticity of ordained life as guided by the example of Jesus—preaching to the poor, releasing captives, freeing the oppressed, and so forth—the *Directory for the Life and Ministry of Priests* encourages priests to "maintain their ministry with a spiritual life to which they give absolute pre-eminence….[T]he priest must enter into a special and profound rapport with Christ, the Good Shepherd, who alone remains the principal protagonist in any pastoral action."[1] *Pastores Dabo Vobis* states the point clearly: Priests must have a sense that "the spirit of the Lord is upon [them]" in order to carry out the mission of Jesus.[2]

According to Father George Aschenbrenner, predicting or evaluating qualities for authentic celibate ministry requires a diverse portfolio of examples. For instance, says Aschenbrenner, while a photo normally reproduces what a camera sees, a portrait "involves shifting shades of light and shadow to communicate the artist's unique view of the subject. Different people paint different portraits of the same thing."[3] Thus, while there is a "changing face of the priesthood,"[4] with conflicting portrayals of the office—sometimes damaging, other times edifying—certain historical portraits can help illuminate a contemporary reflection of the Lucan scene at the synagogue in Nazareth. The ultimate objective of such examination is for seminarians and priests to learn who they are with respect to where they are called to go. As Saint Augustine so aptly put it, we examine ourselves and others with respect to our brokenness—*we see through a glass, though* darkly —so that we can come to a greater awareness of God—*then we see face to face.* In other words, by examining our strengths and weaknesses with respect to the successes and failures of the past and present, we discover who we are, and who we are to become. An awareness of the self allows one to enter more deeply into a life with Christ.

How, then, does one discover a vocation? What are good examples of priestly ministry? All are called to respond to God's call, but not all are called to priesthood. What qualities can help determine an appropriate response to God's invitation?

True Humility

In what has grown into a popular book about a Benedictine monk, Dom Joseph Warrilow, AKA Father Joe, Tony Hendra describes the qualities of the man who saved him from spiritual destruction. According to Hendra, ministers of this sort are humble, authentic, saints.

> A saint is a person who practices the keystone human virtue of humility. Humility in the face of wealth and plenty, humility in the face of hatred and violence, humility in the face of strength, humility in the face of your own genius or lack of it, humility in the face of another's humility, humility in the face of love and beauty, humility in the face of pain and death. Saints are driven to humbling themselves before all the splendor and horror of the world because they perceive

there to be something divine in it, something pulsing and alive beneath the hard dead surface of material things, something inconceivably greater and purer than they.[5]

Modern-day priests have come to recognize the virtue of humility as much more than a cloistered monastic witness. Rather, priests of today are challenged by an injured society that is in desperate need of humble servants in the field. Above all, the faithful seek Christ, and they must find him among savvy, secular, and often indifferent companions. Ultimately, these faithful provide the fundamental reason for service. Like the saints, priests must encounter society with humility and gentle service. Humility is the key to saintliness, and the key to authentic service.

A Good Fit

The examples of the saints have taught us that humility flows from the Spirit, and that there is an intimate connection between a man's response to his vocation and the working of the Spirit. Father Joe's priesthood was described in terms of a well-tailored suit that fits him perfectly, both inwardly and outwardly. It "felt right" and transformed him into a remarkable priest. The "fuel [that] drove his engine" was the fit between his humanity and his priestly vocation.[6] *Pastores Dabo Vobis* reiterates this same image by directing the priest to be "consumed" in his vocation.[7] Pope John Paul II explains that when Jesus said, "The Spirit of the Lord is upon me" (Luke 4:18), he meant that "the Spirit penetrated every part of Him, reaching to His very depths."[8] This same Spirit must touch every priest to the depths of his personality. The Spirit is the "pulse beneath the hard dead surface," and humility flows from this penetrating Spirit.[9]

What is needed for a man to arrive at a sure point that the priesthood is truly his calling, for him a well-tailored suit?[10] Priests must know where they fit into God's purposes. Abraham and Sarah, Moses, David, Isaiah, Jeremiah, John the Baptist, the apostle Paul, Mary the mother of Jesus provide examples of this recognition. They placed their whole life and deepest values in God's hands. A vocation gives a purpose to one's life. It uses one's best gifts. It employs one's genuine values. It brings forth a profound sense of peace. We all have the potential for gifts and talents that can make a difference. A vocation brings these gifts together along with a sense of God's purpose in life.

The word *vocation* comes from *vocare,* a calling to do God's will. God calls you to the place where your deep gladness and the world's hunger meet.[11] A man with no stable sense of self-worth, no sustaining grounding or purpose, no disciplines to cope with isolation and failure, and no centering values to claim will not be able to grasp God's desires for him. If one's biography reads as "gazing and grazing," a priestly vocation will never "fit."

Knowing the Way

Lewis Carroll tells of Alice in Wonderland as she falls precipitously down a well and finds herself lost and frightened. She finally comes to a fork in the road, in the middle of which stands a giant oak tree holding a Cheshire cat. "Which road should I take?" asks the trembling Alice. "Where do you want to go?" queries the cat. "Well…, I really don't know," claims the girl. "In that case," judges the cat, "it makes no difference."[12] Likewise, men without a sense of direction cannot take on a priestly vocation. They cannot discern what avenue would be a good fit in their lives.

Basing one's vocation on the values of the powerful and influential is empty. Some men have agreed to a priestly vocation because of the influence of others, family, social expectations, and so on. This type of person is "other directed," finding his "vocation" in another's desire. Such candidates will inevitably find themselves unhappy and frustrated, following an uninspired, fated path toward harm.

An authentic match between God's call and the needs of the Church finds solid ground when one's "I am"—that is, one's readiness and willingness—is based on self-knowledge and enlightened judgment. The depth of an authentic vocation lies in an awareness that one has been personally called by Jesus. Talents, energies, drives, and gifts are realized only in partnership with God.[13] One does not so much grasp a priestly vocation, as they allow themselves to be lured and awakened to it: "In a vocation we are called to a captivation, a luring toward commitment of our spirit that leads to freedom."[14]

The fifth edition of *The Program of Priestly Formation* underlines this same point:

> [A candidate for the priesthood is one] who has real and deep relational capacities, someone who can enter into genuine dialogue and friendship, a person of true empathy who can understand and know other persons, a person open to others and available to them with a gift of himself and of receiving the gift of others. *This, in fact, requires the full possession of oneself. This life should be one of inner joy and inner security, signs of self-possession, as well as generosity…that is, a person who is free to be who he is in God's design…*[15] (italics added).

Counter-Indicators

No one is exempt from a vocation. "God has a project for each of us, he 'calls' everyone. What is important is knowing how to recognize this call, how to accept it and how to be faithful to it."[16] Part of this process is knowing that there are certain counter-indicators to an authentic priestly vocation, recalling that the best predictor of future behavior is past action. Certain personality types are unable to discern a true vocation to the priesthood:

> *Preoccupied Individuals:* those with a negative self-image, an uncontrollable need for personal closeness, a deep fear of rejection, and a strong likelihood of entering relationships where personal and sexual boundaries are blurred and/or crossed.

> *Dismissive Individuals:* those with a negative view of others, along with an inflated and unexamined self-image and self-

presentation; those who view others as objects, with almost no capacity for empathy, and use compartmentalization (splitting) to avoid honesty and pain.

Fearful Individuals: those with a negative self-concept combined equally with a negative view of others; those driven by fear of rejection and abandonment, and who perceive others as incapable of offering help.

John Paul II wrote of the call of Jesus to his closest disciples Peter, James, and John in the Garden of Gethsemane, "Get up, let us be going" (Mark 14:42). He comments, "Even if these words indicate a time of trial, great effort, and a painful cross, we must not allow ourselves to give way to fear....On another occasion, to the same three disciples, Jesus said, 'Get up and do not be afraid' (Matthew 17:7). God's love does not impose burdens upon us that we cannot carry, nor make demands upon us that we cannot fulfill. For whatever He asks us, He provides the help that is needed."[17]

This courage and ability to follow Jesus can be heard only by those who are not preoccupied, dismissive, or fearful, "to those who obey the call of God and set out, not knowing where they are going" (see Hebrews 11:8). It takes a deeply reflective individual to *set out* trusting God to determine the goal, as did Abraham and Mary. As the pope indicated, "Beginning with Abraham, the faith of each of [us] represents a constant leaving behind of what is cherished, familiar, and personal, in order to open up to the unknown, trusting in the truth we share and the common future we all have in God. We are all invited to participate in this process of leaving behind the well-known, the familiar."[18]

This "setting out in trust" can commence only in those who are brave and capable enough to "put out into the deep (*duc in altum*)" (Luke 5:4). One must not be afraid even when danger lurks and the future is unclear. Becoming and "being" a priest demand true and in-depth *character*. According to Daniel Goleman, character is a quality that permits a person to fully disclose, "Here, I *am*."[19] This identity gives direction to one's life for it has taken deep root in one's soul.[20]

What characteristics are evident when a man possesses the ability to set out into the deep with trust? What constitutes a "wholesome priesthood," a true "zeal" for priestly ministry, not given to fatalism, a patience that encourages one to hold steady, a visionary aptitude marked with a youthful spirit which imagines ideals and does not fear the future, a spirited enthusiasm about all aspects of ministry, and the ability to submit to the mysteries one celebrates?[21]

An authentic call to priestly ministry is heard as a commitment to model Jesus' wholeness. In this way, a seminarian or priest becomes a bridge and not an obstacle in preaching the kingdom of God. If a seminarian or priest is given to omnipotence, omniscience, and omnipresence, he reduces himself to "godlike strivings" and damages or breaks the bridge of human formation.[22]

History and Wholeness

History is of enormous assistance in situating today's seminarian and priest in terms of their ability for wholeness and character.[23] The Council of Trent defined the priesthood in terms of two sacraments: "the power to consecrate" and "the power to forgive sins." The *Constitution on the Sacred Liturgy* (1963) from Vatican II introduced changes that greatly altered one of these staples of priestly life—for example, use of the vernacular, communion under both species, concelebration, and turning around the altars (and the priests).

After Vatican II, the number of those going to communion rose, while the number going to confession dramatically dropped. In 1968, Catholic reaction to the so-called birth control encyclical, *Humanae Vitae*, created a storm of protest that established an emerging pattern of dissent. In effect, "disillusionment on birth control was a harbinger of the future [and] when it became clear that the church's position on celibacy would not change, priests decamped in droves."[24] This disillusionment became more complicated when some trends in moral theology began questioning concepts that had been clear for generations: for example, mortal sin and intrinsically evil acts. The seminary system itself faced great turmoil and change especially from 1967 to

1980. The recent sexual-abuse crisis compromised ecclesial, priestly, and episcopal stability, leading to an era of suspicion. From the 1960s to the present, the priest has moved from being "another Christ" to "the first among equals," creating instability in priestly lives. As fewer men entered seminaries, the number of Catholics continued to grow.

This historical perspective must be placed within the larger framework of the priesthood which emerged. After the Second Vatican Council, priesthood was interpreted from the perspectives of ordained ministry *and* the priesthood of the faithful. Jesus had imparted to the whole people of God the essential tasks of preaching, sanctifying, and shepherding. The common priesthood of the faithful and the ministerial (hierarchical) priesthood are ordered toward each other, and *share* these threefold tasks in their own ways and under the one priesthood of Christ.[25] The laity exercise these tasks in the world, while the priest does so in the church.

Thus the very meaning of ordained priesthood shifted, along with the responsibilities of the faithful. The priest is one who acts "in the person of Christ," but he acts equally in the name of the whole people of God. While the priest stands as guide and illuminator, he is now joined by the whole people of God, co-responsible for the Church.

The fullness of the priesthood resides in the bishop, who, with other bishops, form a college of bishops under the full authority of the pope.[26] Priests form a presbyteral college under the authority of a bishop, and they have the local church as their primary focus. The new schema places the ordinary priest in a somewhat "diminished" light, what Bleichner terms "the symbolic diminishment of the priesthood in the presbyteral order."[27] This historical understanding is important in assisting a seminarian to properly discern a call to the priesthood, and a priest to further understand this call in a post-Vatican II Church.

The shift in the understanding of priesthood brought about by the Second Vatican Council now places a tremendous emphasis on the *character* of a priest. As the person of Jesus literally "suffuses" the Church with his presence, the priest is called in an analogous fashion to celebrate the sacrifice of the Mass by bringing people together in prayer, and to minister to the hungry, thirsty, naked, and imprisoned. Priests must be the "walking symbol of Christ's presence."[28]

Pertinent to the life of a priest, Jesus has given the Church certain marks or beacons which become defining characteristics of their ministry.[29] Priests must exemplify unity, holiness, catholicity, and apostolic origins. These marks form a good checklist for self-reflection and ongoing discernment for seminarians and priests.

- Am I a sign of unity, a bridge, or an obstacle in my responsibilities of preaching, sanctifying, and shepherding?
- Am I a facilitator for unity and charity, rather than hostility and anger?
- Am I a transparent vessel of God's presence?
- Am I an authentic preacher of the Word of God?

Lifelong Conversion

There can be little doubt that the life of a seminarian and priest must be suffused with prayer and contemplation. How else can one form a true priestly identity? Constant *conversion* is a necessary element in discerning priestly character.[30] It is "the gradual, often arduous turning away and withdrawal from sin and selfishness, and the turning correspondingly toward God, the source of goodness and inspiration."[31] Saint Paul is a good example.

> *Not that I have already obtained this or have already reached the goal; but I press on to make it my own, because Christ Jesus has made me his own. Beloved, I do not consider that I have made it my own; but this one thing I do: forgetting what lies behind and straining forward to what lies ahead, I press on toward the goal for the prize of the heavenly call of God in Christ Jesus. Let those of us then who are mature be of the same mind; and if you think differently about anything, this too God will reveal to you. Only let us hold fast to what we have attained.*
> PHILIPPIANS 3:12–16

Conversion is a lifelong process. If one can truly say "I am" at ordination and all the days which follow, one must be in a continual process of conversion. Human conversion involves several dimensions, each of which is important for the health of any vocation. Father Bernard Lonergan, SJ, describes three variations:[32]

Intellectual conversion: The development of new horizons, seeing life in radically new ways.

Moral conversion: Overturning old values, former biases, and negative behaviors, substituting new values, habits of mind and behavior based on perceptions of intellectual conversion.

Religious and grace-filled conversion: Development of a personal and behavioral horizon which moves to a world of knowledge and experience mediated by God, allowing oneself to be led into the hands of God.

The priest is called to be a bridge-builder, a peacemaker, a reconciler, a mediator of unity. Only deep conversion—intellectual, moral, and religious—enables these goals to be achieved. *The Basic Plan for the Ongoing Formation of Priests* stresses the "new identity" priests must achieve as they move along through stages of their priestly life: after ordination, first pastorship and beyond, and finally into retirement. This plan identifies a threefold process—interior, exterior, and celibate—along with the temptations, graces, and discernment that accompany each dimension of the journey.[33] Once again, the idea is that human formation is a lifelong process that involves the whole person (intellectual, religious, or other).

3

The Responders
˝Who Are Today´s Priests˝

In the 1950s and 1960s, U.S. seminarians were largely Caucasian, middle-class, second- and third-generation Catholic, and generally well educated. They came mainly from practicing Catholic families, had attended Catholic schools, and they were imbued with a Catholic ethos (for example, they were taught by religious sisters, steeped in Catholic history and teaching, eager to be priests, and honored for being so). English was also their common language. Seminaries were generally the same everywhere. Once ordained, priests shared a common experience of those ordained before them. When I entered the theologate in 1964, for example, I was using the same textbooks as my priest-uncle when he entered the same seminary in 1929. Fifty years ago, seminaries were overflowing. The teaching was generally superb, especially during high school and college. Seminarians were ordained into a large presbyterate, with good priestly companionship and support. The priest was considered a well-educated and professional man,[1] and his personal foibles and limitations were overlooked in light of the respect given to the priesthood itself. In many American cities the bishop was held in high regard, very often on the same plain as elected officials.[2]

Then and Now

Many studies have been published about the end of this era and the seminarians who now are entering U.S. seminaries. These men will be the Church's future priests. Who are they? The ordination class of 2004 supplies helpful indices. Seminarians are older (median age in the seminary is about thirty-five years old), educated in various fields of study, and more were born outside the country. Catholic University of America sociologist Dean Hoge notes key transitions since 1998.[3]

(1) The average age of ordination rose from about thirty-five to thirty-seven, with 49 percent under thirty-five and 22 percent under thirty years old; 3 percent of the 2004 ordination class was over sixty years old.

(2) The level of education prior to entering the seminary rose. In 1998, 70 percent had a bachelor's degree, whereas in 2004, 78 percent earned this level of degree. In addition, those who received a master's and other professional degrees before entering rose from 13 percent to 28 percent.

(3) The percentage of newly ordained priests in 2004 born outside the U.S. rose from 24 percent to 31 percent. The four principal countries of origin were Vietnam, Mexico, Philippines, and Poland.

Today's seminarians have been involved in various parochial ministries before entering the seminary—as altar servers, lectors, and eucharistic ministers. Over half of these seminarians attended Catholic schools, and about 40 percent attended Catholic colleges. In addition, some grew up in other churches, for example, the Methodist church. Most significantly, most entered the seminary because a priest prompted the vocation.[4]

Profile of Today's Seminarians

Sister Katarina Schuth, O.S.F., of The St. Paul Seminary School of Divinity at the University of St. Thomas, St. Paul, Minnesota, suggests that every seminarian has a unique profile based on family, religious background, previous experiences with the Church, and educational opportunities.[5] According to Schuth, there are several dominant "dimensions of diversity" that shape the identity of seminary candidates. Heritage, education, culture, and church are particularly important.

> *Heritage*: family background, personality and character, place of origin, religious background, age, and health.

> *Education*: natural intellectual abilities, educational background, learning styles, and financial success (or failure).

> *Culture*: racial and ethnic background, cultural experience, language background, and attitude toward culture.

> *Church*: experience of Church, theological/ideological position, spiritual experiences, liturgical experiences, devotional life, and ministerial images and goals.

In light of these four points of reference, Schuth was able to construct a profile of U.S. seminarians from the perspectives of religion, intellect, character, and culture. Ultimately, Schuth's analysis highlights the challenges of modern formation. The following brief examination of each profile sets the stage for subsequent methods of seminary screening.

Religious Profile

About one-third to one-fourth of today's seminarians are deeply rooted in their faith, raised in families who were practicing Catholics, and who happily accept the priestly vocation of their son. They are highly motivated, with a moderate to good grasp of the Catholic tradition.

About one-third have recently undergone a conversion experience. Often seminarians have been away from the practice of the Catholic faith, now called back by significant prayer experiences such as pilgrimages and charismatic involvements. These men may exhibit a type of rigidity born of a desire for security and stability. Some are fearful or vulnerable about losing what they have gained.

About one-fifth of today's seminarians have practiced their faith only sporadically. They did not attend Catholic schools and the seminary is their first religious educational experience. Some seminarians overlap many of these profiles and have come of age after the Second Vatican Council. They have lived their lives mainly under one pontificate, with consequent unswerving devotion to Pope John Paul II. They may sustain a fear of change and a fear of "the world" and see the seminary as a bastion of security. These seminarians often look for a sense of orthodoxy. They may tend to be defensive and fundamentalistic.

Intellectual Profile

A few have benefited from first-rate classical education and have studied philosophy and theological studies before entering the seminary, determined to keep growing intellectually. They understand the relationship between learning and the capacity to minister with integrity.

Most seminarians have a reasonably good college degree and adequate intellectual abilities and are looking for insights into their religious tradition. They tend to integrate study, prayer, and pastoral placements. Some of these seminarians may carry a certain deficiency in studying theology. Their past studies have been in such fields as business, science, and technology, with little exposure to the humanities. They tend not to be readers, and may lack a certain "imagination" to enter into the world of philosophy and theology.

A few of today's seminarians have weak educational backgrounds, with consequent limited ability for reading, reading comprehension, writing, research, and the capacity to use a library. They suffer from a narrow technological education. Some of these seminarians are further burdened by learning disabilities, such as dyslexia and attention deficit disorder. They can too often be thought of as unintelligent, whereas the real problem lies in their inability to study.

Some seminarians lack adequate English skills to enter into philosophical and theological studies and lack an ability to enter into the American educational system (including class participation and written and/or oral examinations).

Some seminarians are "older candidates" and have been away from academic studies for many years, some of whom have never been interested in studying at all. They experience an "urgency" to get ordained.

Character Profile

In light of the basic axiom that "grace builds on nature," *Pastores Dabo Vobis* (43) articulates the basic human qualities necessary for healthy priestly formation. For example, balance in judgment and behavior, freedom, and loyalty. Many seminarians have and continue to develop these qualities, while others have obstacles and deficiencies to overcome. The greatest threat to ministry occurs when deficiencies exist in character structure and internal disposition, rather than as the result of life-circumstances or external attributes. But even certain external liabilities call for clear discernment and judgment—for example, chronic illness, such as diabetes, obesity, addictions, and overly introverted and passive personalities.

Internal and external impediments can be overcome—many of the finest priests endure such ailments—however, seminarians and vocation directors must be particularly sensitive to character flaws and physical disorders that can impede (or terminate) the possibility for effective ministry.

Although internal disposition often marks the success or failure of seminary candidates, external cultural factors must also be taken into account. Unfortunately, modern culture often impedes. For example, individualism limits altruistic motivations, consumerism produces a need for what is newer and faster, and the media's ability to infiltrate all levels of society—especially through the internet—inhibits creativity and can promote dangerous ideologies. These influences are apparent in some of today's seminarians, often infecting their capacity for the basic human qualities outlined in *Pastores Dabo Vobis*.[6]

What Kind of Priest Do We Need?

Modern seminarians are certainly very different from those of previous generations and cultures.[7] Diversity is a permanent characteristic of today's seminarian and tomorrow's priest.[8] *Pastores Dabo Vobis* (17) points out that "the task of ministerial priesthood is to 'help the People of God to exercise faithfully and fully the common priesthood that it has received.'" Certain characteristics of today's seminarians will enable them to perform this task well. They will be capable of dealing with the diversity in the communities they serve. The type of seminarians we admit today will be with us for the foreseeable future.[9]

The seminary itself will need to adapt in light of the changing reality of today's seminarians. Candidates must be formed into mature adults, with healthy support networks. They must sustain an active and committed prayer life. They need to have a good grasp of Catholic doctrine and theology, with an ability to minister and preach well in English. They must possess basic pastoral skills and be capable of accepting the role of pastor soon after ordination. A seminarian must be capable of making a sincere promise of obedience to his bishop, and he must be able to live a peaceful, chaste, and celibate life.[10]

Screening

A great deal has been written about the proper screening and assessment for entrance into the seminary or a religious house of formation. This chapter would be incomplete without some basic points in this area of concern. *Pastores Dabo Vobis* notes the "increasing consensus" regarding the need for preparation *before* entering a major seminary or house of formation. This "propaedeutic" period refers to a program of formal discernment, including education and basic training.[11] It is also the appropriate time for screening and assessment. Overall, the process of evaluation should be seen as a period of insight and self-learning. The critical point is that "the candidate himself is a necessary and irreplaceable agent in his own formation. All seminarian and priestly formation is ultimately self-formation. No one can replace this self-formation in the responsible freedom that we have as individual persons."[12]

The *Program of Priestly Formation* underscores the same point when it indicates that the "admissions process to the seminary seeks to determine whether the candidate has the requisite qualities to begin the process of formation." Assuming a level of "gradualism," which expects more stringent requirements for entrance to the theologate than to a pre-theology program, there remain some basic measures of personal accountability with respect to the "thresholds of human, spiritual, intellectual and pastoral development" of the seminarian.[13]

According to canon law, bishops or religious superiors are ultimately responsible for evaluating a candidate's ability to enter priestly formation. "The diocesan bishop is to admit to the major seminary only those who are judged capable of dedicating themselves permanently to the sacred ministries in light of their human, moral, spiritual and intellectual characteristics, their physical and psychological health and their proper motivation" (*Canon* 241:1). Consequently, the goal of all assessment is to discern a candidate's present ability to be a priest who is open to human, spiritual, intellectual, and pastoral formation.

In *Sex, Priestly Ministry, and the Church,* Len Sperry has brought together the fundamental components for evaluations of the priestly and religious life under three profiles: (1) psychological, (2) psychosexual, and (3) developmental components.[14] While each of these profiles rests on his own insights and study, he leans heavily on the work and observation of others. An overview of these profiles provides helpful guides for assessing the breadth and depth of evaluation protocol.

Basic Psychological Factors

Biological and Constitutional Factors: health history, and status; family history of substance abuse or psychiatric disorders; drug or medication history

Social Determinants and Current Life Situations: family background; educational and work history; friends and social support systems

Identity and Self-Concept: self-view and how one is viewed by others; level of self-esteem, ego-strength; personal and career aspirations

Personality Factors: capacity to work under tensions and deal with multiple stresses; energy level; time management abilities; adequacy of defenses; cognitive functioning; presence and degree of underlying narcissism; capacity to establish and maintain interpersonal relationships, comfort and effectiveness in group settings; capacity for receiving feedback from others; empathy ability; capacity to maintain appropriate boundaries; ability to relate comfortably with authority figures

Sexual Maturity: sexual orientation, identity, and behaviors consistent with a vocation; attitudes toward celibacy; formational growth; potential resistance to growth; and maturation of sexual experience or expression

Requisite Ministry Skills, Capacities, and Experience

Personal Capacities: openness and flexibility; sense of humor; capacity for self-appraisal; adequate etiquette skills; adequate English fluency in reading, speaking, and writing; and familiarity with and attraction to the Roman Catholic priesthood

Interpersonal Capacities: adequate psychosocial development and capacity to relate to all age groups; the capacity for celibacy; and the ability to cope with loneliness and establish healthy, long-term relationships

Basic Ministerial Skills: leadership potential as exhibited in personal initiatives and personal life decisions; capacity to cooperate with others; capacity to communicate adequately in English in both writing and speaking

Ministerial Experience: a commitment to promote social justice; past experience of active involvement in a parish or other Catholic communities; familiarity and experience with ministerial requirements of the sponsoring diocese or religious order

Negative Predictors of Vocational Success

Emotional: self-preoccupation; poor judgment; inability to empathize; overly dependent, or overly defensive

Historical: previous treatment for serious psychiatric disorders; repeated failures; impulsive decision-making; decisions based on intense spiritual experiences

Motivational: any indication that the candidate desires to escape "self," family, or life situations; attraction based on insecurity and wanting to be cared for; or ambitions that overreach one's capabilities

Psychosexual Assessment

Family of Origin
Goal: understand family attitudes about sexuality

Sample Question: How comfortable were family members in discussing sex and sexuality?

Prepubescent Sexual Development
Goals: to understand the individual's earliest sexual feelings and experiences

Sample Question: At what age were you first aware of sexual feelings or your own sexuality?

Sexual-Abuse History
Goals: to determine if any sexual abuse or exploitation was experienced

Sample Question: When you were growing up, did anyone older than you touch you or look at you in a way that was blatantly sexual?

Puberty and Adolescence

Goals: to understand adolescent sexual development, particularly regarding puberty and masturbation

Sample Question: What were your sexual fantasies?

Sexual Orientation

Goals: to understand the individual's awareness of his sexual orientation

Sample Question: Have you ever been curious about or aroused by members of your own sex?

Dating and Adult Sexual Activity

Goals: to understand the individual's experience of dating and adult sexual activity

Sample Question: Have you ever had a sexual encounter with someone you did not know before that day?

Paraphilias and Problematic Sexual Behavior

Goals: to determine if the individual has engaged in sexual deviancy or problematic behavior

Sample Question: Did you ever engage in any sexual behavior that others consider to be unusual?

Current Management of Sexual Behavior and Feelings

Goals: to understand how the individual manages and integrates sexual feelings in light of the celibate lifestyle of a priest

Sample Question: How do you understand and respond to your sexual desires?

Developmental Assessment

Predisposing Stage (prenatal to postnatal)
- Pregnancy and birth experience
- Temperament and mother-infant "fit"
- Hormone levels
- Attachment style
- History of abuse or neglect
- Family functioning and style
- Family attitudes regarding sex

Childhood Stage (1–7)
- Sexual self-exploration
- Self-soothing capacity
- Practice of adult roles
- Gender identity and parental identification
- God-image
- Best friend or confidant

Preadolescence Stage (8–12)
- Same-sex sexual exploration
- Homosexual play
- Heterosexual relational experience
- Sexual attraction, feelings, and fantasies

Adolescence Stage (13–19)
- Sexual exploration or expression
- Sexual orientation
- Capacity for self-mastery
- Capacity for responsibility, cooperation and self-transcendence
- Capacity to establish physical and emotional intimacy

Early Adulthood Stage (20–39)
- Capacity for mature intimacy
- Communicating about intimacy issues
- Capacity for critical refection and critical social consciousness

Mid-Adulthood Stage (40–55)
- Balancing self-interest with self-surrender
- Level of generativity

These psychological, psychosexual, and developmental factors provide guidelines for the assessment of a candidate for a seminary or house of formation. Personal interviews by a trained psychologist are necessary. Assessment interviews should be long enough to enable the psychologist to assess "not only the applicant's overall mental health and stability, but also an applicant's *character*."[15] In some cases this may require more than one session. There is no single test or set of psychological tests (or interviews) that are perfect, but careful and comprehensive results can be achieved by using a variety of testing procedures.

The process of assessment might look like this: An applicant is interviewed by his bishop or religious superior, vocation director, and others appointed for this initial task of assessment. During this time the applicant is introduced to methods and techniques for discernment, or propaedeutic experiences, which allow the candidate to carefully examine his own vocational experience.

During this early stage of inquiry, several necessary documents are gathered. For example, the completion of a diocesan or religious application booklet; a physical examination; a biographical review (via interview or administered form); criminal investigation, including fingerprinting, previous arrests or lawsuits; and letters of recommendation, including letters from other seminaries or religious communities attended.

Only after the successful completion of these first steps should the applicant proceed to clinical testing. Afterward, the professional psychological analysis is presented to the bishop, religious superior, and vocation director, and together they meet to determine if the applicant should move to the next stage of candidacy. Ideally, the candidate is informed of the final decision and its reasons—positive and negative—and he should be given the opportunity to meet again with the psychologist and vocation director in order to receive helpful insights regarding his testing, interview, and backgrounds checks.[16]

If a positive judgment is made, the candidate moves forward to the application process for academic study, including information about his academic history and appropriate graduate entrance exams. The overall process places the candidate into a propaedeutic context and gives the applicant the opportunity for personal insight. He can understand why he *is* or *is not* an acceptable candidate for priestly formation at this point in his life. The assessment process must aim to promote an ever deeper consciousness of the candidate's own identity.[17]

Tests for Behavioral Assessment and Psychological Profiles

Melvin C. Blanchette provides one of the most comprehensive lists of testing available for seminary or religious applicants.[18] The tests fall into two categories: (1) objective instruments, which evaluate measures of intelligence, reasoning ability, mental functioning, and general personality, and (2) projective instruments, which provide information about a person's unconscious personality and defense mechanisms.

Objective Instruments

Wechsler Adult Intelligence Scale-Revised (WAIS): determines overall competency which enables an individual to comprehend well and deal effectively with challenges. It is now in its fourth edition and is a standard IQ test. Should impairments be detected here, further tests are available.

Reitan Screening Test: examines level of competency in receptive and expressive language skills. The test is comprised of a diverse collection of thirty-two items that require the testee to demonstrate abilities such as naming, reading, writing, spelling, arithmetic, identifying body parts, identifying and copying shapes.

Bender Gestalt Test: consists of an analysis of nine geometric designs. Scores demonstrate the perceptual tendencies to organize visual stimuli into configural wholes (*Gestalten*) and are useful for detecting normal or abnormal brain function. Each design is presented sequentially to the subject whose task is to reproduce them on a blank sheet of paper.

Minnesota Multiphasis Personality Inventory-2 (MMPI-2): helps diagnose mental dysfunction by reflecting the type of disorder and the intensity of the problem. Nine main scales of personality have been developed, although there are a host of subtexts: hypochondria, depression, hysteria, psychopathic deviation, masculinity-femininity, paranoia, psychasthenia, schizophrenia, and hypomania. MMPI-2 is the most frequently used objective personality test in current practice.

Million Clinical Multiaxial Inventory-III (MCMI-III): provides information to clinicians who must make assessment and decisions about persons with emotional and interpersonal difficulties. The MCMI-III provides critical interpersonal data, such as problems in the area of human sexuality.

Projective Instruments

Sentence Completion: explores targets areas such as self-concept, identity, family background, emotional maturity, developmental tasks, affective dynamics. The *Loyola Sentence Completion Blank for Clergymen* is currently the best instrument in use for seminarians and clergy.

Rorschach Inkblots: this test explores an individual's relational style; particularly whether or not the person is aware of color and human movement.

House, Tree, Person: this instrument provides a window into how a person completes an unstructured task.[19]

Summary

Each applicant has the right to his own good name and confidentiality. It is critical that every diocese and religious community have written parameters about such concerns. These written guidelines should be discussed with the applicant at the beginning of the propaedeutic experience. In light of new canonical guidelines, judgments must also be made as to how long these tests are considered valid, and how long they are to be kept in an applicant's file. Record keeping and confidentiality must remain within the guidelines of the *Ethical Principles of Psychologists and Code of Conduct*. Finally, the candidate must give written consent for the release of information to the bishop or religious superior, vocation director, and seminary admissions personnel.[20]

To maximize the benefit of these interviews and tests, the applicant should be given a gentle, respectful, and professional verbal analysis of the various processes he underwent. The trained psychologist should give this assessment whether or not the applicant has been accepted to the diocese or religious community.

This chapter has viewed the overall "types" and cultural groups currently applying for the priesthood in dioceses or religious communities. These profiles help to set the formative agenda for seminaries and houses of formation. The entire goal of psychological testing is to maintain the guiding principle in *Pastores Dabo Vobis* that a candidate's personal history is the single most reliable means of assessing human maturity, especially because it takes into account diverse cultural backgrounds.[21]

A candidate must have the ability to do priestly work and accomplish this responsibility with human wholeness and integrity. One of the gifts of the Church is that of "reception" (*recipere*, from the Latin, "to take in, accept, adopt"): "a process whereby the faithful accept a teaching or decision of the Church....Believers affirm a teaching or practice through steady observance…in the living spirit of *commun-ion*."[22] Every candidate for the priesthood must possess a capacity to be a receiver of the Church's tradition recognized in a constant growth-pattern of maturity and personal integrity.

4

Human Formation
˝Who You Are and Who You Should Be˝

Pastores Dabo Vobis (PDV), the U.S. Bishops' fifth edition of the *Program of Priestly Formation (PPF)*, and *The Basic Plan for the Ongoing Formation of Priests (BPOFP)* all underscore "the fundamental place of human formation" in priestly formation. Two guiding principles set the stage for this discussion: first, the sage advice of Ignatius of Antioch that only in heaven can one "be fully a human being,"[1] and second, that "becoming good" is the central object of being human.[2]

Formation Markers

The *PPF* and the *BPOFP* point out that formation is primarily cooperation with the grace of God. Human development aims at making one's humanity a bridge for communicating Jesus to others. Seminarians and priests must be men of communion who cultivate their capacities as listener and speaker.[3]

The *PPF* gives helpful guidelines about the meaning of human formation. Like the *BPOFP*, it focuses on Jesus Christ, the one who is *the* bridge between God and humanity. The humanity of the seminarian and priest must serve this same goal. The *PPF* offers nine objectives for becoming this bridge.

A seminarian and priest must encompass the following traits:

1. a man of communion
2. a good communicator
3. a prudent and discerning person

4. a person of affective maturity
5. one who respects, cares for, and has vigilance over his body[4]
6. one who can take on the role of a public person
7. a free person—to be who he is in God's design
8. a person of solid moral character with a firmly developed conscience
9. a good shepherd of material possessions

These human qualities provide the basis for a threefold process of self-knowledge, self-acceptance, and self-gift, all within a context of personal spirituality. The *PPF* suggests that every seminary should develop "markers of human formation." In other words, for example, seminaries could develop measurable criteria for determining the development of students with respect to the nine objectives above. Such formation "markers" help the seminarian, faculty, and formation team to identify growth or setback, and they set a standard to be followed after ordination. Ultimately, seminarians and priests bear the primary responsibility for their own human formation and the necessity of demonstrating evident signs of maturity. They should continually evaluate themselves with respect to their capacity to embody the ministry of Christ.

"Markers of human formation" should not be interpreted as hurdles to overcome;[5] rather, they should be interpreted as indicators of one's commitment to authentic human development. An understanding of the promise and pitfalls of humanity leads to a deeper awareness of God. Following the advice of the earliest Christians, we realize that we are made in God's image, and looking inward helps to uncover the Spirit that continues to form us. As seminarians and priests mature, their understanding of their own humanity breeds confidence and authenticity in every aspect of their life. They are better able to present themselves; to use their gifts of learning and culture to empower those around them; and to defend themselves from challenges outside their control.[6]

Lifelong Formation

Achieving the wisdom and confidence of modeling Christ is a lifelong process. Propaedeutic and seminary formation are only a few of the many stages of maturity. The *BPOFP* insists that ongoing human formation must be a "permanent" part of a priest's life.[7]

The notion of "permanence" has different dimensions depending on the various stages of priestly life: the beginning years, transition years, facing changes in assignment, becoming a pastor, the midlife years, and the older and senior years.[8] As suggested by its title, *The Basic Plan for the Ongoing Formation of Priests* describes a plan for what priests can expect as they mature in their ministry; the tasks, temptations, and challenges they will face; the graces offered; and the type of discernment needed. It is important to recognize that no two priests mature in the same way, much less respond to the same circumstances in the same way. The personal identity of a priest depends on personality and temperament, coupled with individual discernment. In any case, authentic, lifelong priestly formation leads to a fulfilling and rewarding experience of ministry.[9]

Human formation is a progressive achievement, a lifelong pilgrimage.[10] Seminarians and priests are *always* preparing themselves. We noted already the cultural diversity of today's seminarians and priests. In *The Interpretation of Cultures*, anthropologist Clifford Geertz defines culture as "a historically transmitted pattern of meanings embodied in symbols, a system of inherited conceptions expressed in symbolic forms by means of which people communicate, perpetuate, and develop their knowledge about and attitudes toward life."[11] In this sense, one's progress in human formation and development is intrinsically cultural and always in process. The Emmaus story (Luke 24:24–35) stands as a centering point of reference as Jesus is the formator who walks the pilgrimage with the disciples until they fully experience and recognize him. Surely this takes a lifetime.

With respect to human formation, seminarians and priests must desire perseverance, permanence, and continued commitment. This presumption comes only after a certain level of human maturation has happened.[12] This experience is not a playacting ruse, but a recognition of readiness deep within a person's heart which is revisited and rekindled.

The Inner Light

Historical, sociological, and psychological studies offer an instructive picture of today's seminarians and tomorrow's priests. In light of the sexual scandals and the changing demographics of today's Catholic population, these studies present a portrait of priesthood that challenges formation leaders—bishops, vocation directors, and so forth—to make critical judgments about the applicants offering themselves as candidates. Even before the recent sexual crises, the vast majority of local churches, seminaries, and religious communities were already progressing in the use of professional psychometric and psychological testing and interviews.[13]

The fifth edition of *The Program for Priestly Formation* sets the stage for a proper understanding of human development. This foundation finds an important complement in *The Basic Plan for the Ongoing Formation of Priests*.[14]

The task of these programs (*PPF* and *BPOFP*) is not easy. As noted above, no two seminarians or priests are alike, and no two formation settings share the same background and development. C. K. Chesterton noted that human life comprises a complex problem that calls for a complex answer.[15] By virtue of the complex nature of humanity, formation is very difficult to harness. Harold S. Kushner describes the complexity this way:

> A rabbi asked his students, "How can we determine the hour of dawn, when the night ends and the day begins? One student suggested, "When from a distance you can distinguish between a dog and a sheep." "No," was the rabbi's answer. A second student said, "It is when one can distinguish between a fig tree and a grape vine." "No," the rabbi replied. "Please tell us the answer," the students asked. The teacher said, "It is

when you look into the face of a human being and you have
enough light *in you* to recognize them as brothers and sisters. Until then it is night and darkness is still within us.[16]

The day arrives when a candidate brings all of his discernment to
a specific bishop, religious, or seminary community, and articulates
his desire, "I want to be a Catholic priest." His human formation has
long been in process. Now he faces a series of tests to see if his desire
finds an ecclesiastical resonance. Does he have enough light in him to
further develop his initial foundation?

This "light" is fundamental. It is the meaning of Saint Irenaeus'
insight that the glory of God is the fully alive human being. Ronald
Rolheiser comments:

At the deepest level of our being, we already know beauty
and resonate sympathetically with it because we are ourselves
beautiful. In the depth of our souls we carry an icon of the
One who is Beautiful. We have within us the image and likeness of God, the source of all beauty. That *Imago Dei*, that
place where hands infinitely more gentle than our own once
caressed us before we were born, where our souls were kissed
before birth, where all that is most precious in us still dwells,
where the fire of love still burns, and where ultimately we
judge everything as to its love and truth; in that place, we feel
a vibration sympathetique in the face of beauty....It stirs the
soul where it is most tender.[17]

If the seminarian or priest is not in contact with his inner light
and goodness, he will never adequately care for souls in his priestly
work. Daniel O'Leary observes:

The vocation of the priest is to be a prophet of beauty, to
remind people of the light within them....The calling of the
priest, like it was for Jesus before him, and like it is for the
Church and her sacraments now, is not to introduce some-

thing new to God's creation, but to reveal, purify, and inten-
sify what is already there.[18]

In other words, the call to the priesthood is an invitation to discover the grace that God has planted within us. The call opens the
path to light, to Christ, to the Spirit that guides formation. Helping
seminarians discover this inner light is often complicated and difficult. It demands authentic reception and docility on the part of the
seminarian. It requires hard and discerning work on the part of the
formators.[19] Rules can be dictated, courses can be learned, pastoral
skills can be incorporated, but human formation is a grace that calls
for desire and reception. The best candidate in a formation program
acknowledges that he does not *have* to be a priest, even though he
deeply longs to be. Such candidates are open and willing to learn, to
be formed, and to value new insights.

If the day arrives when it seems best that a seminarian departs
from the seminary or formation program, it should be understood as
a "good day." It is a day of insight and even deep joy: the candidate
"sees" that the call he discerned is not going to work out in his life for
any number of reasons—usually complicated, but often life-giving.
This clarity is also not a private affair between the person and Jesus,
but rather a publicly ratified certitude on the part of the Church. Seminarians who are formed in this way understand and move on with
peacefulness. Those who do not comprehend their unsuitability for
priesthood often struggle for many years—sometimes for life—and
they find themselves in constant pangs of anger and blaming others.

The Root of Human Formation

The meaning of authentic human formation in a priest is as old as the
First Letter to Timothy (3:2–4):

> *[A] bishop must be above reproach, married only once, tem-*
> *perate, sensible, respectable, hospitable, an apt teacher, not a*
> *drunkard, not violent but gentle, not quarrelsome, not a lover*

of money. He must manage his own household well, keeping his
children submissive and respectable in every way.

In other words, bishops or priests ought to have passed a certain threshold of human development.[20] This fact should be evident in their demeanor and behavior. This is the point in *Pastores Dabo Vobis* (nos. 43–44): "The whole work of priestly formation would be deprived of its necessary foundation if it lacked a suitable human formation."

Vatican II's *Lumen Gentium* (no. 8) describes the humanity of Jesus as the living instrument of salvation (*vivum organum instrumentum*). This critical point is reiterated in *Pastores Dabo Vobis* (no. 43). A seminarian and priest must mold his human personality in such a way that it becomes a bridge for others in their meeting with Jesus. In the process of human formation, it is necessary that a candidate discover a true sense of autonomy, where slowly but surely he understands the events and relationships of his life and what has formed him—a process that is enabled by God's grace, proper motivation, and direction.[21]

Jesus called his disciples with an invitation, "Follow me" (Matthew 4:19). The command sets the pattern for all discipleship. Jesus is calling seminarians and priests to go beyond themselves and move into uncharted waters. To accomplish this, they need a certain level of personal freedom to begin this mission. This invitation or call is always individual, touching deeply the human and spiritual dynamism of a person.[22] Seminarians and priests must not think that spirituality automatically changes their humanity. They must be transformed and undivided, living lives free from compartmentalization.[23]

Only an authentically human individual makes a good priest and truly assures "faithful, zestful service in a diocesan (or religious) priestly vocation, something far more attractive and compelling than sheer survival."[24] To heed Jesus' call means a "sea change in a man's life,"[25] allowing "follow me" to be a fire deep within.

Monasticism of the Heart

How does one develop this kind of authentic humanity? One essential component is the experience of solitude.[26] Only when seminarians and priests learn to be alone and honest with God can they lay the foundation of human development. In other words, they must develop a "monasticism of the heart"[27] in order to anchor their humanity and priesthood against stormy times. Solitude becomes a "tap root" for active ministry and gives awareness to the relationship one has with Jesus.

The "experience of solitude" demands, as Arnold Toynbee insisted, a pattern of "withdrawal and return," a time in the desert and a time in active ministry. This process must develop into a habit for every seminarian and priest, a habit that necessarily manifests itself in changed attitudes.[28] The habit of "withdrawal and return" demands "a real willingness to 'leave all' for the sake of prayer, study and involvement in the pastoral lives of people."[29] Human formation requires the habit of rest.[30]

Formation From Within and Without

The primary task in human formation of seminarians lies within and without.[31] That is, seminarians must continually monitor and shape themselves from within, striving for physical and psychological maturity. At the same time, however, the seminarian must accept formation from without: the influence of their formation team, peers, and their experience of prayer. Indeed, seminarians experience all of the formative elements of the Church of Christ. "[Formation] is the necessary assistance of the Church community…that leads [a seminarian and priest] to the fullest possible restoration of the likeness of God in his person, his human nature….The seminarian's formation should teach him to learn to live as a free man, but a free man of faith."[32]

Complete formation from within and without requires seminarians and priests to live integrated lives. They must strike a balance between personal and communal experience; between culture and Church; and between human conversation and prayer. The seminary (and diocese or religious community) must provide certain integrating experiences to help seminarians and priests to grasp that authentic human formation leads one toward holiness of life.[33] Human formation, including all its internal and external dimensions, fosters a common bond with the presbyterate and religious community. James J. Gill, SJ, noted that the lack of an integrated life ultimately leads to "casualties" in formation.[34]

Priestly Spirituality

The primary focus of this book is on human formation, but it is also important to say saying something about its interrelationship with priestly spirituality. The spiritual formation of seminarians and priests is an essential part of their development, a deep realization that "God's love has been poured into our hearts through the Holy Spirit that has been given to us" (Romans 5:5).

John 21:15–17 presents a crucial context for priestly spirituality:

> *Jesus said to Simon Peter, "Simon son of John, do you love me more than these?" He said to him, "Yes, Lord; you know that I love you." Jesus said to him, "Feed my lambs." A second time he said to him, "Simon son of John, do you love me?" He said to him, "Yes, Lord; you know that I love you." Jesus said to him, "Tend my sheep." He said to him the third time, "Simon son of John, do you love me?" Peter felt hurt because he said to him the third time, "Do you love me?" And he said to him, "Lord, you know everything; you know that I love you." Jesus said to him, "Feed my sheep."*

In other words, all priestly spirituality is based on the love of Jesus. The *Decree on the Ministry and Life of Priests* from Vatican II states this point clearly when it indicates that priests attain holiness of life and exercise their ministry faithfully only when they do so "in the

Spirit of Christ" (no.13). *Pastores Dabo Vobis* further stresses that just as the Spirit of the Lord came upon the Messiah and filled him, so too must this same Spirit pierce the life of a seminarian and priest (no. 19). Only when this occurs will the spiritual existence of the priest be marked by a holiness of life. Saint Augustine taught that a priest's heart must manifest "pastoral charity" as his very ministry is an office of love to care for God's people. Through holiness of life, the priest realizes that the Spirit of God is upon him and that he is authentically acting *in persona Christi* (no. 33).

Spiritual Renewal of the American Priesthood (1973) defines basic Christian spirituality as "the living out in the circumstances of one's daily life the dying and rising of Jesus."[35] The circumstances of the life of today's seminarians and priests bear unique characteristics. There are declining numbers of vocations. Permanent deacons and laypeople fulfill many ministerial responsibilities. Sexual scandals, the increased rate of divorce among Catholics, and deep polarizations are signs of the times that demand clear spiritual priorities for seminarians and priests. This spiritual precedence must be nourished by daily prayer and meditation, celebration of the Eucharist, a spiritual director, a support group, a balanced life, and an authentic commitment to one's diocese or religious community.

These priorities must be accompanied by a regular celebration of the sacrament of reconciliation. In Luke 5:1–11, Peter and his companions had been fishing all night long with no results. Everything looked hopeless. Jesus told Peter to "put out into the deep water and let down your nets for a catch." When the nets were tearing due to the large catch, Peter's reaction was clear: "Go away from me, Lord, for I am a sinful man!" Here one finds a sincere confession, a moment of humility, openness to God's grace. Seminarians and priests should make Peter's confession a model. In this way, one will become more sensitive to Paul's claim that "by the grace of God I am what I am, and his grace toward me has not been in vain" (1 Corinthians 15:10).

It is easy for anyone to become absorbed by the external stimuli of television, radio, internet, and noise. We must strive for internal silence to gain Peter's humility. In his *Rule*, Saint Benedict indicates that in silence we demonstrate our true place before God. We learn to "be still" (Psalm 46:10). Seminarians and priests must seek opportunities for silence to walk in God's presence and under God's protection (Genesis 17:1).

Edward J. Farrell offers an example:

> One evening as the priest walked along the country road he came across an old man out enjoying the twilight air. They walked and talked together until a sudden rain made them take shelter. When their conversation moved into silence, the old Irishman took his little prayer book and began praying half aloud. The priest watched him for a long time, then in a quiet whisper said, 'You must be very close to God!' The old man smiled very deeply and answered, 'Yes, God is very fond of me.'"[36]

Authentic human formation and development will only occur in a deep spiritual context, rooted in silence and a personal relationship with God.

5

Human Sexuality
˝Definition and Evaluation˝

Perhaps never before in the history of the Church has there been so much ferment as there is now about issues of sexuality. Awareness of the sexual-abuse crisis has raised serious issues which must be carefully assessed and addressed. A balanced definition of human sexuality is needed to guide our inquiry:

> [Human sexuality] is our way of being in the world as gendered persons with self-understandings as male or female, bodily feelings and attitudes, affectional orientations, capacities for sensuousness, and with a drive toward intimacy and communion.[1]

In its 1983 document *Educational Guidance in Human Love*, the Congregation for Catholic Education put it this way:

> Sexuality is a fundamental component of personality, one of its modes of being, of manifestations, of communicating with others, of feeling, of expressing and of living human love. Therefore, it is an integral part of the development of the personality and of its educative process (no. 4).[2]

It is not possible to make a serious and knowledgeable commitment to a chaste and celibate way of life if human sexuality is not understood and properly appropriated in one's life.

Types of Sexuality

Sexuality can be perceived from a threefold perspective: *primary sexuality*, referring to our embodiment as males and females; *genital sexuality*, which includes the dimensions of sexual fantasies, longings, desires, urges, and physical responses in our bodies, accompanied by more or less strong urges for sexual behavior; and *affective sexuality*, which includes feelings, moods, and acts that move toward another to express closeness and intimacy.

These three aspects of sexuality must not be confused. For example, a healthy affective sexuality demonstrates qualities such as warmth, tenderness, gentleness, sensitivity. A serious problem arises when one confuses genital and affective sexuality, believing that genital sex is the only way of being intimate with another person. Many men—particularly in young adulthood—often mistake sexual intensity with intimacy.[3] Those committed to living celibately must develop an authentic spirituality of their sexuality in order to fully live the three dimensions of human sexuality. [The celibate's deepest sexual hunger must be for human fulfillment developed over a lifetime of prayer and authentic friendships with others.] Human isolation is dangerous, too easily leading to the fragmentations of such dysfunctional behaviors as pornography and sexual acting out.

[The celibate, as with every person, must develop an affective sexuality, learning to be peaceful with one's aloneness and becoming absorbed in the quest for one's deepest self.] The basic need in a celibate's life should not be genital sex, but rather intimacy, relationship, affirmation, and acceptance. Sexual maturity, therefore, is "not a state to be achieved, but a process to be lived."[4] The Irish Benedictine Mark Patrick Hederman wrote, "Love is the only impetus that is sufficiently overwhelming to force us to leave the comfortable shelter of our well-armed individuality, shed the impregnable shell of self-sufficiency, and crawl out nakedly into the danger zone beyond, the melting pot where individuality is purified into personhood."[5] In other words, seminarians and priests must live and love in the world. They must allow relationships to shape their understanding of God, and in so doing, they will be able to step outside their own limitations. Saint Thomas Aquinas taught that love "melts the heart: that which is melted is no longer contained within its own limits, quite the contrary of that state that corresponds to 'hardness of heart.'"[6]

It is critical for anyone pursuing and living a life of chaste celibacy to appreciate how love fits into the celibate life. C. S. Lewis wrote:

> To love at all is to be vulnerable. Love anything, and your heart will certainly be wrung and possibly be broken. If you want to make sure of keeping it intact, you must give your heart to no one, not even an animal. Wrap it carefully round hobbies and little luxuries; avoid all entanglements; lock it up safe in the casket or coffin of your selfishness. But in that casket—safe, dark, motionless, airless—it will not change. It will not be broken; it will become unbreakable, impenetrable, irredeemable. The alternative to tragedy, or at least to the risk of tragedy, is damnation. The only place outside Heaven where you can be perfectly safe from all the dangers and perturbations of love is Hell.[7]

- Love
C.S. Lewis

The temptation of celibates is toward a love that is universal and vague. Celibates must love particular people, some with deep friendship, learning to integrate these loves into our identity.[8]

In *Sex, Priestly Ministry, and the Church,* professor of psychiatry Len Sperry offers helpful guidelines to understand and situate human sexuality.[9] Sperry's descriptions enhance and enliven the definition of human sexuality already given. One's sexuality has a biological and genital component, the first referring to one's maleness or femaleness, and the latter referring to one's behavior: that is, what we think and do sexually. Human sexuality is a process of making sex significant in our lives. It does not have to include genital intercourse or related sexual practices. Sexually healthy persons view their sexuality in positive terms. They are comfortable and emotionally responsible with their sexuality.

Important Distinctions

Sexual orientation refers to the emotional and erotic feelings for a category of people: heterosexual (the opposite sex), homosexual (the same sex), or bisexual (a desire to relate sexually or intimately with both women and men).[10] One's sexual orientation is normally set before mature choice is possible.

Sexual identity refers to one's self-identification as heterosexual, homosexual, or bisexual, as well as one's subjective sense of being a man or a woman. While sex is a biological designation (male or female), gender is a socially constructed designation (masculine or feminine).

Gender role is the set of social and cultural norms, attitudes and behaviors expected of a man or woman in a given cultural context. Before one is even conscious of the fact, individuals usually internalize these expected roles and behaviors.

Deep friendship is achieved when one maintains a close personal relationship with another person. For a celibate, friendship is the capacity to share one's life with another without being married or violating chastity. Only authentic friendship with God enables true friendship.

Asexuality is a quasi-sexual orientation.[11] This "orientation" refers to individuals who deny or are uncertain about their sexual orientation. Such persons should not be admitted to seminary or formation programs. They are often unable to create authentic friendships and may sexually act out later in an attempt to discover their sexual orientation. These persons fear closeness, intimacy, and commitment and maintain interpersonal distance. They are sometimes referred to as *hyposexual.*

Intimacy is a special kind of relationship that involves promoting closeness, warmth, and affection in human relationships.

Intimacy requires equal sharing of respect and a reciprocal expression of one's thoughts, feelings, and sentiments. As persons share joys, hurts, and fears, they develop committed, close, and lasting intimacy. "Communication of personal values, respect for personal feelings, acceptance of personal limitations, affirmation, sharing of hurts and fears of being hurt, and forgiveness of errors constitute the 'spiral of intimacy.'"[12]

Barriers to Intimacy include the inability to distinguish sex from intimacy, lack of trust, a sense of self-entitlement, poor boundaries, lack of self-esteem, and impaired communication. Certain skills and insights are helpful in developing a healthy celibate intimacy: self-knowledge (Saint Teresa of Ávila wrote that "almost all problems in the spiritual life stem from lack of self-knowledge"), comfort in being alone, the conviction that God loves me, a joyful willingness to serve and minister, an ability to be self-disclosing when appropriate, a capacity to be a brother to everyone and a spouse to no one, and an ever-deeper awareness of one's generativity, modeled by the celebration of the sacraments, praying, teaching, and all sorts of ministerial responsibilities: that is, one must ask, "Am I truly building up and giving birth to the people of God."

Common problems contribute to one's inability to maintain true intimacy with others: fear of abandonment and betrayal, fear of loss of autonomy and self, fear of closeness, fear of engulfment, fear of damage, strains of sexuality that neutralize tenderness (need to dominate, inflict harm), self-defeating, masochistic behavior (need to be punished), inability to idealize, overidealization, inability to trust, and increased expectations of relationships. In summation, these problems generally "involve fears of being hurt, inability to trust, emotional difficulties, or unrealistic expectations."[13]

Cultural Implications

Cultural factors play a critical role in the development of one's sense of human sexuality. It is important to note the main ingredients in this multicultural mix since so many of today's seminarians and priests come from non-Western and non-American cultural backgrounds. It would be misleading to imply that some overarching rubric can portray every culture. Still, there are some elements that can be sifted from multicultural studies on human sexuality. These studies indicate that certain family units within particular cultural groups tend to carefully guard their sons in order to preserve them for priesthood. This familial protectiveness can cause some seminarians to limit their relationships or friendships with women. This is particularly evident in seminaries where some international students have difficulty dealing with women advisors or mentors. Generally, these men have had limited sexual education, with an equally narrow awareness of their own development. Human sexuality is usually a topic that is not discussed in such cultures. Sexual transgressions are interpreted as bringing shame on the family. This cultural factor can lead to "saving face" by hiding the truth and sometimes lying.[14]

> *Vietnamese* seminarians and priests come from traditional families with a strong hierarchical structure. Most have had virtually no social or dating experiences, and if the family believes a son has a priestly vocation, he is watched and guarded with great care. What he "possesses" must be shielded. When he enters the seminary, this watchfulness grows in intensity. Vietnamese parishioners sometimes act as an extended family protecting the seminarian from any sexual dangers that might damage his progress to ordination. Homosexuality is also considered a grave transgression. Should a Vietnamese man sense this orientation, he will hide or deny it, trying to avoid the heavy burden of humiliation. Some experience troubling inner struggles as a way of coping with sexual illiteracy and frustration. In the United States, Vietnamese

women seek higher education to get better and higher-paying jobs, but not to become leaders or role models in the family. This factor dramatically affects the way a Vietnamese seminarian and priest relates to women.

Hispanic seminarians and priests generally learn about sexuality from others and usually not from their parents. Boys pick up the notion of *machismo* and its typical hierarchical attitude toward women. Women are often seen in a double role of virgin and seductress. Hispanic seminarians normally do not transfer this viewpoint to female faculty or formators. Some of these seminarians talk about their sexuality only gradually. Trust needs to be established before mature conversation takes place.

Filipino seminarians and priests have been greatly influenced by American culture and its attitudes about sexuality. Parents do not normally speak about sexuality to children. Learning takes place usually from friends. Filipino schools now teach about human sexuality. This factor is significant in helping Filipino seminarians and priests to have knowledge about sexuality. Catholicism greatly impacts this culture. Attitudes and behaviors tend to be in line with Catholic teaching. Homosexuality is considered a serious sin.

Asian seminarians and priests come from heterogeneous cultural groups with varied perspectives on human sexuality. However, studies have uncovered several common features. While celibacy is held in very high regard, as is the family, it is expected that a male will marry and have children. Hence strong motivations must be evident when choosing a celibate lifestyle. There is virtually no education about sexuality and a certain naiveté results. The culture(s) expects men to be virgins when they are ordained. There is an apparent shyness to speak about one's sexuality. Sexual transgressions are generally overlooked if they are done discretely.

African seminarians and priests emerge from a culture where family pride is of utmost importance. The mother's role is to introduce children to questions of sexuality, directly with girls, and more indirectly with boys. Because the culture is dominantly patriarchal, a man without a child is seen as a source of shame for not passing on the family name. Celibacy is not considered an important value. Men in this culture are more comfortable talking about sexuality one-on-one rather than in a group. An African girl is not considered a woman until she bears a child, and an African boy is not thought of as a man until he impregnates a woman. Cultural belief places a great deal of strain on upholding the importance of chastity and celibacy for a seminarian and priest.

Three Critical Concerns

Three concerns are critical in preparing today's seminarian and priest to live an authentically chaste and celibate life.

First, sexuality is not simply a matter of intellectual formation; it is a matter of public formation with clear appropriation of sexual values. Sexual formation cannot remain only in the private forum of spiritual direction, but must also have a place in the public forum, including advising and mentoring.[15] Sexuality and celibate sexuality must be on the private *and* public agendas of formation. A seminarian is preparing to be a public person in the Church and the Church has a right to know that the priest being ordained is sexually mature. Peter Rutter convincingly demonstrated in his 1986 landmark book, *Sex in the Forbidden Zone*, that no amount of intellectual training about sexuality is sufficient unless it is accompanied by a capacity to interiorly recognize the true meanings of human sexuality, especially its negative sides such as sexual abuse.[16] In a seminary and formation context, the anthropological, psychological, sociological, and theological/moral dimensions of sexuality and celibate sexuality must be fully treated.

Second, with respect to the above analysis of multicultural

seminarians and priests, formation leaders must be attentive to the various degrees of shame that often accompany dysfunctional sexuality. Shame prevents a person from seeking necessary help or even discussing the matter with a spiritual director. It is vital that seminary formation teams work sensitively with seminarians who experience a sense of shame, a feeling that often borders on self-loathing. Shame is a deeply-felt sense that one does not measure up, and perhaps never will, to the person one had hoped to be. It is experienced as a vague disgust with oneself. This self-loathing takes many forms, for example, some feel as if they are fake, or feel that if people really knew them, they would have contempt for them, or perhaps they seldom feel any real joy.

Persons who experience shame often believe in the false messages that arise from a false sense of self. Shame-prone people discount their positives, judge themselves by unrealistic ideals, translate what they do into who they are, and read their shame into other people's minds.[17]

Third, the role of women in seminary formation is crucial. In the classroom and as formators, women play an extraordinary role in helping students to interact well with women in pastoral, liturgical and spiritual settings.

Taking a Sexual History

It can be beneficial for a seminarian and priest to take a sexual history (see Appendix Two).[18] A sexual history is not a genital history but rather a careful and reflective look at one's psychosexual journey. A threefold purpose guides this undertaking: to assist one to better understand and evaluate one's psychosexual life, to help one to better understand and integrate one's psychosexual history in order to form and develop a healthy and balanced person; and to gain the self assurance of understanding one's psychosexual health. The person taking a sexual history should have access beforehand to the questions to be asked and pursued.

A sexual history must be administered by a trained professional and should be kept in an internal forum in order to guarantee the utmost confidentiality and comfort level for the candidate or priest. Seminary and formation houses often have different testing schedules: for example, some conduct the psychosexual history as part of one's entrance requirements, or after a pastoral year, or before ordination to the diaconate, or sometimes before first profession. In any case, it should be strongly encouraged for every seminarian during the course of his formation.

Seminarians and priests should be encouraged to share the results of their sexual history with their spiritual director for further discernment and judgment. Proper administration of the test should invite candidates to pursue further means for understanding their growth (or lack of growth). For example, the psychosexual history and subsequent analysis may provide a necessary segue to further professional counseling. Most importantly, however, the psychosexual history provides the candidate with critical data to make an informed decision about his formation direction.

In *Sex, Priestly Ministry, and the Church,* Len Sperry offers a certain model for developmental stages of celibacy.[19] *The Basic Plan for the Ongoing Formation of Priests* gives useful guidelines about formation at different stages in a priest's life.[20] The stages of priestly development are often identifiable by specific markers or milestones of celibate life. For priests, these markers can offer helpful insights about a proper time to take a sexual history. For seminarians, they serve as benchmarks for ongoing formation. A sexual history is particularly helpful when seminarians and priests struggle through key phases of their psychosexual development. The reasons for their struggles are often rooted in their psychosexual history.

A sexual history provides the optimum possibility for affective/sexual human integration in order to ground and enhance sensitivity to others, self-understanding, intimacy, openness to others, and compassion. The overall goal is the living of an authentic life of chaste celibacy. Seminarians and priests are not asexual, and they need to be aware of themselves as persons with sexual feelings. They must always act with personal and professional responsibility. When seminarians or priests cross sexual boundaries, they generally inflict incalculable moral, spiritual, psychological and even, in some cases, physical harm.

Seminarians or priests that act out with sexually deviant behavior end up abusing those in their care, and they injure the heart of the Christian message. They become a countersign to the public and their commitment to be chaste and celibate. Every seminarian and priest should utilize the sexual history as a viable and helpful tool to assist them to be more fully human. See Appendix Two for a sample sexual history.

Homosexuality

The clergy sex-abuse crisis raised questions about a possible relationship between homosexuality and the sexual abuse of minors. Clarity on this issue is important.

Homosexuality refers to a "predominant, persistent, and exclusive psychosexual attraction toward members of the same sex. A homosexual person is one who feels sexual desire for and sexual responsiveness to persons of the same sex and who seeks or would like to seek sexual fulfillment of this desire by sexual acts with a person of the same sex."[21] The *Catechism of the Catholic Church* teaches that "Homosexuality refers to relations between men or between women who experience an exclusive or predominant sexual attraction toward persons of the same sex."[22]

In 1996 the Congregation for the Doctrine of the Faith (CDF) issued the *Letter to the Bishops of the Catholic Church on the Pastoral Care of Homosexual Persons*. This document teaches that "[a]lthough the particular inclination of the homosexual person is not a sin, it is a more or less strong tendency ordered toward an intrinsic moral evil; and thus the inclination itself must be seen as an objective disorder."[23]

In light of this teaching, some judge persons with a homosexual orientation to have a "disorientation" toward homogenital acts. The *Catechism* teaches that persons do not choose to be homosexual. The *Letter to the Bishops* teaches that "[t]oday, the Church...refuses to consider the person as a 'heterosexual' or a 'homosexual' and insists that every person has a fundamental identity: the creature of God, and by grace, His child and heir to eternal life."[24]

Modern anthropological and scientific research has unearthed certain considerations about the phenomenon of homosexuality.[25] Three approaches dominate discussion: determinist, constructionist, and interactionist.

Determinist Hypothesis

One school of thought is called determinism: individuals have no free will because their choices and actions are predetermined. Responsibility for one's sexual orientation, say the determinists, is an illusion. Advocates of this "nature" (not "nurture") stance claim that sexual orientation is caused by biology. Contrary to this hard-line approach, most researchers in the scientific community believe that the origins of human behavior, including sexual orientation, are variously determined and involve some measure of choice or decision. This school of thought concludes that "while individuals have certain inclinations to homosexuality, bisexuality, or heterosexuality, the inclination is not a choice, but the individual has a choice as to what to do with the inclination."[26]

Constructionist Hypothesis

Advocates of constructivism adhere to the postmodern stance that all knowledge and identity are relative. In other words, all meaning is socially constructed. This implies that definitions or interpretations of the self—such as sexual orientation—have no basis in physical reality. Homosexuality, then, is not constructed by biology, but generated by culture. For the strict constructionist, reality and power emerge through language. The physical body is merely "raw material" for the social construction of selfhood. Selfhood, in turn, is as pliable as culture and it is not predetermined biologically. According to this view, heterosexuality and homosexuality are not determined by genetics, but by culture and choice. Homosexuality, say constructionists, is the result of "nurture" (not "nature").

Interactionist Hypothesis

According to modern analysis, it is likely that both biology and social construction contribute to one's "selfhood." That is, some combination of nature and nurture appears to be operative with respect to defining sexual orientation. According to this so-called interactionist view, all people are heirs to certain predispositions, but these "natural" tendencies do not preclude the ability for responsible choices in one's life.

In the wake of the sexual-abuse crisis, theories of sexual orientation (nature versus nurture) can sometimes lead to misperceptions about human sexuality and the priesthood. Strict interpretations of one theory over another have fooled many into affirming arguments that do not have true premises. Confusing risk with cause, many wrongly assume that homosexuality is a precursor for pedophilia (or ephebophilia), or even that ordination causes homosexuality and/or pedophilia. Take, for example, the judgment of Dr. Martin Kafka, a member of the study group commissioned by the Vatican in its investigation of clergy sexual abuse:

> We described [homosexuality] as a risk factor [in the sexual abuse of minors]. A risk factor is not a cause. There is, however, a subgroup at risk. Since priests who abuse minors tend to perform most such acts within five to seven years after ordination, being recently ordained is another risk. That does not mean that being recently ordained 'causes' abuse, any more than homosexuality.[27]

Seminarians, priests, formation leaders, and bishops must understand the various dimensions of homosexuality in order not to confuse it with other different biological and social orientations (such as pedophiles, ephebophiles, or rapists) and to determine how—or if—homosexuals can be integrated into priestly formation.[28]

Homosexuality and the Priesthood

The Congregation for Catholic Education released a statement concerning the integration of homosexuality in priestly and religious life.

> The Church, while profoundly respecting the persons in question, cannot admit to the seminary or to holy orders those who practice homosexuality, present deep-seated homosexual tendencies or support the so-called "gay culture." Such persons, in fact, find themselves in a situation that gravely hinders them from relating correctly to men and women. One must in no way overlook the negative consequences that can derive from the ordination of persons with deep-seated homosexual tendencies.[29]

The Congregation discourages discrimination and encourages respect and sensitivity. Ultimately, however, the Congregation warns formation teams to guard against individuals who display deep-seated, disordered tendencies. In other words, like their policy against sexually active heterosexuals, these new norms are meant to protect the Church from homosexuals that are most likely to act out sexually.

Temperance and Fortitude

Morality comes from within and contributes to human fulfillment. Christian anthropology regards the person as composed of body and soul, insisting on the basic goodness of every individual. Authentic human formation involves a movement from what is less to what is more in one's life. When Thomas Merton was about to enter the monastery, he was troubled about his old self, the person he had always been. He struggled to establish a new person, one he wanted to be. He reflected that the old person must die to allow the new person to truly live. This challenge faces every individual and certainly the seminarian and priest.

The virtues of temperance and fortitude are particularly important to help in this process of growth. Temperance helps one to control one's appetites in terms of food, intoxicating drink, and the use of sexuality. Those with self-control enjoy power and strength of character and the peace of heart that comes from exercising temperance. Temperance helps us moderate our attractions and provides a needed balance in our lives. It ensures self-mastery over instincts and keeps desires within the limits of what is honorable and prudent.

The virtue of fortitude or bravery disposes one to do the "hard thing," to pursue "the more," as Ignatius of Loyola indicated. Fortitude arises from an inner courage that helps us overcome our weaknesses and be committed to self-sacrifice for the purpose of authentic humanness. Fortitude ensures constancy in one's life to always pursue the good, to resist temptations, and to overcome obstacles in one's life.[30] Temperance and fortitude help us to walk steadily according to the authentic desires of our heart. Saint Augustine puts it this way: "To live well is nothing other than to love God with all one's heart, with all one's soul and with all one's efforts; from this it comes about that love is kept whole and uncorrupted….No misfortune can disturb it….It obeys only God and is careful in discerning things, as not to be surprised by deceit."[31] When temperance and fortitude have been properly developed, passions can be controlled, and the quality of one's character becomes dependable.

The Role of Friendship

There can be no moral or spiritual life without healthy friendships.[32] One grows good in the company of friends who also want to be good. Good friends share dreams and possibilities while they care for, encourage, and support one another. True friends are not hesitant to help and correct one another. Ultimately, friendship is a moral enterprise.[33] A seminary and religious community, as well as a diocesan presbyterate, must actively foster an atmosphere where personal character is developed and deepened, where seminarians and priests are deeply committed to loving God and one another in a wholehearted manner.

Friendship demands certain qualities of character, such as

generosity, thoughtfulness, a capacity to care, an unselfish willingness to respond to the needs and well-being of others. True friendship avoids manipulation and isolation. Perhaps the traditional condemnation of "particular friendships" was not so much a matter of concern about homosexuality, but rather a hope that the development of friendships not be narrowed to only one person. We become good in company with others who also want to be good.

Exclusivity

Unfortunately, some friendships are unhealthy and actually impede maturity, fostering exclusivity and divisiveness instead. Such friendships involve a high degree of self-preoccupation, whereby individuals do not seek or offer counsel outside their own small group. Such relationships hinder human development, true community, and presbyteral and religious fraternity.[34] Seminarians and priests often enter into these types of relationships to seek security, to fill an affective void, and to compensate for past or present hurts and wounds. Some of these uncompromising friendships are very damaging to a seminary or religious community, especially when such friendships comprise, for example, associating only with others in one's ethnic group. This is a problem which creates divisiveness and hinders apostolic charity.

Three subtypes of exclusive friendships are similarly destructive:

1. *Possessive* friendships are built on emotional preoccupation and manipulation.
2. *Complaining* friendships are built on chronic dissatisfaction and criticism.
3. *Impairing* friendships are formed around dependency, idealization, and control. They often lead to destructive behavior toward one another.[35]

All of these destructive friendships are based on personal need rather than character. Seminarians and priests are called to a communion-of-life and must not fall into a type of radical individualism which is essentially solitary, disconnected, and autonomous. Humans, by nature, are not isolated and fundamentally private. Human identity and freedom emerge from community. Friendships with others draw us out of ourselves, give us life, and lead us to communion with others. Isolated seminarians are not qualified to engage the unavoidable communal life of Jesus' ministry.

Infatuation

Immature individuals often mistake infatuation for friendship. Infatuation is an unreasoned or extravagant passion or attraction to another. Like most exclusive relationships, it is based on the need to complete or fill some void in character, some unfulfilled longing or desire. Unfortunately, most infatuation is one-sided, whereby one individual assumes power over another. Infatuated persons are vulnerable to manipulation and control. Infatuation is not always sexual, but it can assume its worst form when it is. Church documents have often referred to "disinterested friendship" as a way of cautioning against infatuation and perhaps illicit expressions of sex. "Disinterested" should *not* be interpreted as cold or isolated. Rather, disinterested friendship means involvement and care without becoming exclusive.

What qualities of character are needed to avoid infatuation and develop healthy, "disinterested" friendships? First, generosity of spirit, a fundamental unselfishness to expend ourselves for others; second, a noncalculating spirit that reaches beyond egocentrism and narcissism; third, true empathy to enter into the viewpoints, values, and desires of others; fourth, a receptivity to make room for others in one's life; fifth, a vulnerability to the cares, interests, and concerns of others; and sixth, a fidelity to the time it takes to develop trust and confidence in others. In other words, any relationship that violates the gospel emphasis toward community is in danger of becoming a destructive, exclusive hindrance to formation.

Types of Friendship

Aristotle spoke of three kinds of friendship: usefulness (centered around common tasks or projects), pleasure (centered around people we enjoy being with), and character (centered on a mutual desire for virtue). We cannot do without any of these types. Friendships of character, however, are particularly essential to personal growth and maturity and they demand both permanence and availability. Character friendship is the most perfect and complete type of friendship. Character friendship demands a certain level of self-transcendence and teaches us to care deeply for others. It is the bedrock of good ministry.

The development of character friendship helps the seminarian and priest from becoming disenchanted and disillusioned with one's vocation, and provides an arena for healthy criticism and correction. We need others who value what we value and whose presence reminds us of our vocational commitments. By spending quality time with good friends, we develop in virtue and moral excellence. Friendship constitutes a distinctive way of life where we develop a habit-for-companionship. True friendships are essentially a conscious calling to others for a Christlike behavior. Character friendship is a matter of helping others grow in the gospel values of humility, patience, perseverance, impassioned justice, exquisite love, and bold courage. Friendship implies benevolence: "To be benevolent in spiritual friendship involves encouraging one another in prayer, supporting one another during times of hardship and trial, and challenging one another to avoid the perils of complacency and mediocrity. To be benevolent in spiritual friendship is to be willing to receive the hopes, dreams, worries, fears, and even failures of the other into our heart as a sacred trust and to respond with the compassion, love, and encouragement of Christ."[36]

Loneliness

We are all called to lives of community, but we must also accept the times when God speaks to us in isolation. From the example of Jesus in the desert, we learn that being alone can provide great strength for communal living. But when unchecked and unrehearsed, loneliness makes us vulnerable to temptation and it can hinder our ability to reach out with love to others.

In *The Restless Heart*, Ronald Rolheiser situates loneliness in the deep, restless disquiet every person experiences. In other words, to be human is to be lonely.[37] Loneliness is a felt suffering that can lead to creativity or to destructive and dehumanizing behaviors. It affects all human beings. It is not a cause for shame or a sign of weakness. It is dangerous only when it is not recognized, accepted, and worked through creatively.

Loneliness can never be fully satisfied in personal friendships. Only God can fill our deepest longings. Loneliness demands a journey inward, a degree of interiority and solitude. When we feel lonely, we are being calling to spend time with God. If one is acting immaturely, it may be a result of not spending enough time with God.

In *The Ascent of Mount Carmel*, Saint John of the Cross explains that human affectivity becomes inordinate when one's loneliness operates with no checks.[38] We permit ourselves to enter into a process of self-destruction. Weariness and frustration drive us into a flurry of intense activities. We become tormented by an abiding pain. We feel emptiness at the center of our being. We become darkened and slowly lose our way. We see the world as distorted and negative. We become weakened, lukewarm, and we sink into despair. Nothing can bring true peace without accepting our loneliness, a restlessness satisfied only when our heart rests with God.

Every seminarian and priest must become peaceful and comfortable with the feeling of loneliness. Its darkness and disquiet can be an opportunity for growth or destructiveness.[39] John of the Cross wrote, "O dark night, my guide, more desirable than dawn."[40] Loneliness is a dark night that calls us to contemplation rather than activity. Loneliness is a call to be still with oneself and God. We must not hide from or evade it.

Some believe that personal loneliness can be completely eradicated. This illusion can lead to dysfunctional and dangerous behaviors. Henri J. M. Nouwen explains:

> When our loneliness drives us away from ourselves into the arms of our companions in life, we are, in fact, driving our-

selves into excruciating relationships, tiring friendships, and suffocating embraces. To wait for moments or places where no pain exists, no separation is felt, and where all human restlessness has turned into inner peace is waiting for a dream world. No friend or lover, no husband or wife…will be able to put to rest our deepest cravings for unity and wholeness.[41]

Boundaries

Seminarians and priests must studiously develop proper limits or boundaries in terms of ministerial and professional relationships with others.[42] Professional boundaries are the limits that allow for safe relationships (for example, between peers; teacher and pupil; priest and parishioner). Boundaries safeguard intrusions into one's sphere of safety—what many refer to as "personal space." If priests, for example, exploit relationships to meet personal needs (for example, intimacy or money), or allow themselves to be exploited, they are breaching professional boundaries. Boundary violations usually start from selfish, noncommunal decisions intended to compensate for some deficiency. Those who violate boundaries disregard the safety or well being of others, focusing instead on their own needs.

Certain key characteristics or actions usually precipitate boundary violations. Some seminarians and priests cross boundaries in search of caretakers to make them feel better about themselves. Others engage in activities with ulterior motives: for example, the priest who invites someone on a trip with the real hope of a sexual liaison or a seminarian who befriends a wealthy person in the hope of gaining money. Unfortunately, those who mask their intentions are usually so good at it that they can even fool themselves. Still others cross boundaries because they cannot defend themselves against being drawn into a relationship. That is, out of fear they become overly passive and allow others to take advantage of them. In addition, some seminarians or priests take advantage of others for the purpose of self-gratification: for example, interrogating people in order to discover their sexual orientation. These are just a few of the many subtle (and not-so-subtle) actions that can spell disaster for any vocation. Many of these markers are manifested in the form of harassment.

Harassment

A seminarian and priest must uphold exceptionally high standards in terms of boundary relationships. This need has doubtlessly increased since the sexual-abuse crisis. Harassment of every kind must be avoided. It is illicit and unlawful. In general, harassment can be defined as follows:

> *Verbal harassment:* includes jokes, epithets, slurs, negative stereotyping, unwelcome comments about an individual's body, color, physical characteristics, appearance or abilities.

> *Visual harassment:* includes offensive or obscene photographs, calendars, posters, cards, cartoons, drawing gestures, displays of sexually suggestive or lewd objects, unwelcome notes or letters or any other written, graphic, or electronically transmitted materials that denigrate or show hostility or aversion toward an individual because of a protected characteristic such as race, color, national origin, religion, ancestry, gender, age, or mental and physical disability that is placed or circulated anywhere in the seminary, living space, or workplace.

> *Physical harassment:* includes physical interference with normal work, impeding or blocking movement, assault, unwelcome physical contact, staring at a person's body, and threatening, intimidating or hostile behavior.

Clear strategies need to be adopted to avoid boundary violations: always be professional; be accountable to someone for your behavior; develop a healthy personal life; maintain self-awareness by consistently monitoring your motives, thoughts, attractions, and feelings; and avoid all risky activities such as taking minors on trips without other adults being present.

Moving Forward

As mentioned at the beginning of this chapter, human sexuality is our way of being in the world as men and women. It is, in a word, unavoidable. Human sexuality involves all the things that make us who we are: our character, history, capacity for growth, intellect, ability to love, and much more.

Seminarians and priests must be attentive to the promise and pitfalls of human sexuality. Understanding its various types (primary, genital, affective) and the many distinctions within it (orientation, identity, gender, deep friendship, and so forth) should help those in formation to identify common problems so that they can continually shepherd healthy relationships. Formation leaders should understand these sexual types and distinctions within the context of the many cultural dimensions of modern seminary life. To do otherwise is to invite disorder and sexual crisis. Fortunately, the sexual history can help seminarians, priests, religious, and formation teams during any phase of formation (seminary to retirement) to assess sexual development.

As public persons, seminarians and priests must be particularly sensitive to their own wants, needs, desires, aspirations, and so forth. This means understanding and embracing one's sexual orientation with respect to celibacy. Knowledge of the "science" of sexual orientation should help seminarians and priests discern how (or if) they can thrive as sexual celibates, and such knowledge will equip them to defend themselves against the prejudice and misunderstanding that exists in society today.

Above all, human sexuality deals with relationships. It is part of the human core of love. Thus, it affects our friendships (exclusive or nonexclusive), our ability to deal with loneliness, and our judgment of others. In short, human sexuality is one of our conduits to knowing others, to knowing God. Ultimately, human sexuality provides access to the mystery of God's love for us and, as such, it should be scrutinized and utilized as a vital tool in ministry. Greater knowledge of sexuality—for seminarians, priests, religious, and laypeople—will help the Church move forward.

6

Human Sexuality
"Problematic Issues"

H uman sexuality is one of our strongest God-given gifts. It emerges
from our core and it is at the heart of our relationships with one
another. As relational beings, sexuality is part of what empowers our
response to God.

Unfortunately, like most powerful gifts, human sexuality can be
abused, overused (or underused) to the detriment of others. Inten-
tional or not—nature or nurture—misguided sexuality can inflict
serious harm upon self and others. The discovery and response to the
clerical sexual abuse of minors provides tragic proof of the need for
all people to remain attentive to the grace and power of sexuality,
especially for those in public ministry. Seminarians and priests do
not consciously desire to be obstacles to the proclamation of Jesus in
the Church. However, at times, personal issues give birth to critical
dysfunctions.

This chapter highlights some of the most significant findings and
challenges for modern seminarians and priests with respect to their
sexuality. Here, we explore some of the difficult facts of the sexual
abuse of minors, culpability, the bishop's response(s), penalties, restrictions, important distinctions, dangerous signs, and a variety of
other related challenges in human sexual formation.

Sexual Abuse of Minors, Analyzing the Data

Recent studies have uncovered the tragic scope of abuse within the
Catholic Church in the United States. Numerous reporting agencies—

private and public—continue to research the history and ramifica-
tions of sexual abuse. There are also many media sponsored surveys,
such as those conducted by the *Washington Post, New York Times, Wall
Street Journal, NBC News,* and *Boston Globe,* to name just a few, that
have advertised their findings about the sexual-abuse crisis. In short,
the data can be dizzying, conflicting, and sometimes inaccurate. In an
effort to assess the situation, the U.S. bishops have collaborated with
the John Jay College of Criminal Justice to formulate two critical reports: (1) "A Report on the Crisis in the Catholic Church in the United
States" and (2) "The Nature and Scope of the Problem of Sexual Abuse
of Minors by Catholic Priests and Deacons in the United States." The
John Jay College study presented the empirical data and the review
board supplied an interpretative analysis.[1]

According to these studies, the percentage of priests accused of
sexual abuse versus the total number of priests during the past fifty-
two years is about 4 percent. During certain stretches of this time frame,
however, the percentage of accusations fluctuated drastically. The largest number of offending priests were ordained in the years before and
just after Vatican Council II. The crisis reached epidemic proportions
in the 1970s. In the ordination class of 1970, for example, one priest
in ten would eventually face allegations of sexual abuse. The number
of known allegations declined sharply among those ordained during
the next two decades (1980s and 1990s), and the number is even
smaller today. Since these crimes are often underreported, the actual
average percentage might be higher than these reports indicate.

Although various reporting agencies sometimes provide conflicting data, there is consensus from within and without the Church that
the abuse was significant enough to wound the credibility of the
priestly office. In 2004, Pope John Paul II said that "grave scandal is
caused with the result that a dark shadow of suspicion is cast over all
the very fine priests who perform their ministry with honesty and
integrity, and often with heroic self-sacrifice."[2]

During any crisis, data is critical for reaching proper judgments.
Among the more credible facts and figures of the crisis are those of
researcher Thomas G. Plante, professor of psychology at Santa Clara

University and adjunct clinical professor of psychiatry at Stanford University.[3] In addition to confirming some data from the John Jay College and the National Review Board, Plante discovered some particularly enlightening facts about the abuse of minors. For example, about 5 percent of priests have had sexual experiences with minors, a percentage consistent with estimates for male clergy in other religious denominations, but still too high. About 80 to 90 percent of these offenders engaged with adolescent boys between thirteen and seventeen. This indicates that contrary to popular belief, young acolytes or students (prepubescent youths under the age of thirteen) were not abused nearly as often as older adolescents. It is also interesting to note that the vast majority of priests who sexually abused minors did not commit their first offense until after ordination. This seems to indicate, for example, a deficiency in the sexual formation and/or evaluation of seminarians.

Unfortunately, it is not possible to reprint or reanalyze all of the data concerning the sexual-abuse crisis. However, it is critical for seminarians and priests to engage in such due diligence with respect to the sexual-abuse crisis. That is, they must understand all local and universal church policies for the protection of children. As explored above, all seminarians and priests must continually engage in ongoing formation. Research can help empower them to guard themselves and the laity from further abuse. A good starting point is the research initiated by the U.S. bishops.

The Church's Response to Sexual Abuse

In response to the emerging facts of the crisis, on June 14, 2002, the bishops of the U.S. adopted the *Charter for the Protection of Children and Young People* (hereafter *Charter*), and *Essential Norms for Diocesan/Eparchial Policies Dealing with Allegations of Sexual Abuse of Minors by Priests, Deacons, or Other Church Personnel* (hereafter *Essential Norms*). The bishop's *Charter* and *Essential Norms* acknowledge the recent "crisis without precedent," and they address the enormous "pain, anger, and confusion" that has surfaced in recent years. They continue to seek healing for the tremendous hurt inflicted upon innocent victims and their families and they are working to resolve the bureaucratic secrecy in the Church that enabled the abusive behavior.

The *Charter* presents seventeen articles intended to protect victims and promote healing. For example, the articles provide provisions for outreach to victims (article one); the establishment in every diocese of review boards (article two); no confidentiality agreements (article three); mandated reporting and cooperation with public authorities (article four); the "single act of sexual abuse of a minor—past, present or future—will result in the permanent removal of a priest or deacon from his ministerial duties" (article five); diocesan policies must be clearly publicized and communicated (articles six and seven); the establishment of national Offices for Child and Youth Protection (articles eight through ten); and numerous other provisions to protect the faithful (articles twelve through seventeen), particularly the careful screening of seminary candidates (article thirteen); and full cooperation with the apostolic visitation of seminaries in the U.S. (article seventeen).[4]

The *Essential Norms*, in conjunction with the articles of the *Charter*, present the process to be followed if a credible allegation of sexual abuse of a minor is made against a priest or deacon. The process is intended to identify sexual abuse, penalize offenders, protect the public, and promote healing for the victims.

What Counts as Sexual Abuse?

The *Charter* makes no distinctions in the range of activities which count as sexual abuse (for example, showing sexually explicit pictures or sodomy). In other words, any confirmed violation is a complete violation; there is no sliding scale of punishment. In addition, the *Charter* understands a single act of sexual abuse of a minor as having the same degree of importance as repeated acts of sexual abuse.

Sexual abuse means contacts or interactions between a child and an adult when the child is being used as an object of sexual gratification. A child is abused whether or not this activity involves explicit force, involves genital or physical contact, is initiated by the child, or whether or not there is a discernible harmful outcome.

A sexual act must be external, performed with sufficient internal deliberation and freedom to be gravely imputable.

> [S]exual abuse shall include any offense by a cleric against the Sixth Commandment of the Decalogue with a minor as understood in CIC, canon 1395 §2, and CCEO, canon 1453 §1 (Sacramentorum sanctitatis tutela, article 4 §1).[5]

> If there is any doubt whether a specific act qualifies as an external, objectively grave violation, the writings of recognized moral theologians should be consulted, and the opinions of recognized experts should be appropriately obtained (Canonical Delicts, p. 6). Ultimately, it is the responsibility of the diocesan bishop/eparch, with the advice of a qualified review board, to determine the gravity of the alleged act.[6]

Ultimately, much of the logic behind the Catholic response to sexual offenses is rooted in the interpretation of the sixth commandment of the Decalogue.

Violations Against the Sixth Commandment

In Catholic moral tradition, the sixth commandment has been used as an umbrella term for every sexual sin. A short treatment of this history is helpful.[7]

In the Bible, adultery came to be equated with any type of covenant infidelity. Adultery was referred to as "the great sin" (Genesis 20:9; 39:9). The condemnation of adultery forbade sexual relations with another's spouse. Because true discipleship demands going beyond mere obedience to the law, which means embracing a life of virtue, adultery also became associated with other sexual behaviors that are at odds with Christian living. Thus, for example, to look lustfully at a woman was viewed to be as wrong as the physical act of adultery itself (Matthew 5:27–28). In other words, one's heart is to be the locus of moral thought and behavior. Jesus used the word *adultery* to reject the hypocrisy of outward observance which did not flow from the center of a person (Matthew 12:29; 16:4). Paul also announces that "the night is far gone" and we must conduct ourselves "as in the day." The biblical authors make it clear that the inner center of our morality must not be focused on the flesh, but on Christ Jesus. "Make no provision for the flesh, to gratify its desires" (Romans 13:11–14).

During the first and second centuries, this biblical approach was still evident, for example, in the *The Didache*, the first letter of Clement, and the *Shepherd of Hermas*. In these writings one finds a clear sense that personal integrity demands distance from everything that could obstruct one's path to God. For example, one should avoid slandering, vile and impure embraces, drunkenness, rioting, filthy lusts, detestable adultery, disgusting arrogance, and many other vices.

Patristic writers placed great emphasis on idolatry as the most fundamental human sin. Marital sex for procreation was the only kind of blameless sex, although, according to Saint Augustine, even marital sex is inferior to complete abstinence. Medieval authors such as Saint Thomas Aquinas applied the sixth commandment to whatever was opposed to the virtue of temperance. He was one of the first to cite the sixth commandment as a catchall for all types of sexual sins. Subsequent writers emphasized, for example, the cleric's relationship to Christ as a marriage which forbade any type of sexual union as a form of adultery.

This abbreviated history provides a backdrop for understanding why the Church teaches that a cleric who abuses a minor commits a sin against the sixth commandment.[8] Such priests commit a sin of adultery against their marriage with Christ. The fathers of the Council of Trent (1545–1563) developed a moral theology of sexuality based on the claim that adultery results from the failure to pursue chastity in all its forms. All forms of impurity and immodesty, therefore—internal and external—were condemned. This teaching led to the prohibition of venereal pleasure outside the context of marriage, which was only intended as a means for preserving procreation.

Eventually, restrictions on sexuality and pleasure became official

Church teaching. A sexual act was considered unchaste or impure if it was done for the sake of genital pleasure. The teachings of the magisterium in the nineteenth and twentieth centuries continued this tradition. The Church emphasized to an even greater degree the prohibition of sexual acts which, of themselves, frustrated the natural procreative end of sexuality. By the end of the twentieth century, Catholic moral tradition officially forbade sexual acts outside marriage because any such act would entail genital pleasure without respect for the procreative and unitive dimensions of human sexuality.

Recent moral theology places greater emphasis on a theology of the person. Pope John Paul II, for example, focused less on "the intrinsic nature of sexual acts" than on the importance of the spousal significance of the human body. One must not frustrate the procreative dimension of the sexual act, not primarily out of fidelity to its natural end, but rather out of respect for the dignity of the person whose body was created in a nuptial way. Chastity demands that personal dignity always be respected.

Overall, the moral tradition can appear very complex with respect to the history of the interpretation of the sixth commandment. While adultery was condemned in the Bible, the term eventually included a more comprehensive understanding of sexuality, that is, any sexual acts that were understood to frustrate the dignity of the human person. Genital sex between a married person and someone other than the spouse counts as an explicit act against the sixth commandment. All other sexual sins are implicit offenses.

James H. Provost writes, "Diocesan bishops, church administrators, and ecclesiastical judges are faced with a serious responsibility to interpret sins and crimes 'against the sixth commandment of the Decalogue' carefully, strictly, and in keeping with the limitations placed on those who would impose penalties in the Church."[9] In the *Essential Norms*, this "serious responsibility" translates into written policies and a review board comprised of competent persons to advise bishops in their assessment of allegations of sexual abuse of minors.[10] Only a bishop has the ultimate right to judge whether or not a cleric has offended against the sixth commandment. If he judges that a cleric has sexually abused a minor, moral responsibility is presumed, and the church punishes the cleric with fitting penalties.[11]

Penalties: Repair, Restore, and Reform

"No one is punished unless the external violation of a law or precept, committed by the person, is gravely imputable by reason of malice or negligence."[12] The intent of sexual gratification is an essential element in assessing the situation. The *Charter* assumes that there is always some level of sexual gratification on the part of the abuser.

A penalty is imposed for three reasons. To *repair* scandal, *restore* justice, and *reform* the offender.[13] This threefold penalty is meant to promote healing. It calls for fraternal correction. Justice and charity demand that an offending priest be assisted toward necessary moral and spiritual reform. According to Pope John Paul II, "[E]ven while recognizing how indispensable these criteria are, we cannot forget the power of Christian conversion, that radical decision to turn away from sin and back to God, which reaches to the depths of a person's soul and can work extraordinary change."[14]

Heeding this advice, the bishops recognize the possibility for the healing and conversion of perpetrators. However, in the wake of the crisis, they also take a hard line with respect to restoring justice and preserving the safety of victims when abuse has been identified.

No Tolerance

When even a single act of sexual abuse by a priest or deacon is admitted or is established after an appropriate process in accord with canon law, the offending priest or deacon will be removed permanently from ecclesiastical ministry, not excluding dismissal from the clerical state.[15] The *Essential Norms* specify that violators will not be permitted "to celebrate Mass publicly, to wear clerical garb, or to present [themselves] publicly as a priest[s]."[16]

Who to Blame, Who to Punish?

Subjective culpability refers to the personal and moral responsibility of the offender. If, for example, an adult fondles the genitals of a child, it is presumed that the adult is subjectively and morally responsible for this act and commits a grave sin. Subjective culpability is not present if it is clear that personal responsibility is not possible—for example, when actions are performed while under the influence of drugs or alcohol, or when one is impaired by a chronic sexual disorder. Nevertheless, any sexual abuse of a child—under any circumstance—is still a violation of the sixth commandment and qualifies as an "objective" sin. According to the Catholic moral tradition, objective sin can occur even in the absence of subjective culpability.

Despite this tradition, some still ask why the Church imposes penalties on priests who are *not* subjectively culpable for their abuse. The *Essential Norms* state, "At all times," an offending cleric is held responsible for his actions because sexual abuse "is a crime in the universal law of the church and is a crime in all jurisdictions in the United States."[17] If a violation of the sixth commandment occurs objectively, even without subjective culpability, the victims remain wounded, and the offenders must face penalties. In other words, when sexual abuse of a minor occurs, it is always an objectively grave evil and thus subject to punishment.

Removal From Ministry

During a bygone era, the hymn *You Are a Priest Forever* typified the Catholic attitude toward priests. Once a priest, always a priest! The hymn's words carry a meaning which assured that newly ordained priests would always carry the sacramental anointing of the spirit. Externally, the ordained priest is commissioned to celebrate the sacraments and visibly witness to priestly ministry. Internally, he is configured to the person of Christ as priest, prophet, shepherd, and king. According to the *Decree on the Liturgy*, when a priest celebrates the sacraments, Christ is present.[18]

When a priest is permanently removed from public ministry, this removal affects the "external" meaning of his priesthood. However, such censure can never erase the interior configuration to the priesthood of Christ. The priest who is removed from public ministry carries an unimaginable wound since his interior priestly meaning cannot be fulfilled in an external fashion.

We have already witnessed the removal of priests from public ministry. This reality changes their lives and the lives of their brother priests. It affects the morale of priests and the laity, but it is necessary in cases of sexual abuse.

Resignation From Ministry

Resignation from ministry may be a pastoral solution to this difficult problem. A priest who might consider resigning from ministry is the one who has suffered a loss of credibility through consistent or singularly egregious compromise of his human and priestly integrity. He has compromised himself and his priestly vocation. At this point, not only is the priest suffering but also the integrity of the Church. Scandals have occurred in other professions and ways of life—for example, physicians, teachers, psychologists, counselors, coaches, scout masters. Clerical scandals receive greater attention and raise deeper emotions due to the nature of a priestly vocation.

Resignation from ministry is a possible option for some priests who have fallen victim to human frailty, weakness, and addiction(s) while ministering in the Church they hoped to serve. "More often than not, what gives way first is the priest's inner life, and then the quality of his personal life and ministry."[19] Resignation from ministry is not intended to scapegoat or ostracize priests and bishops who compromise their priesthood. Rather, it is meant to offer a viable resolution for a chronically wounded healer.

In his 1999 study of sexual abuse by Roman Catholic priests, *Bless Me Father for I Have Sinned*, Thomas G. Plante remarks, "It takes more than simply cognitive readjustment to alter basic drives."[20] Priests with clear psychological and psychosexual and/or criminal problems must seek the possibility of rehabilitation. If this is not possible, due either to the priest's personal unwillingness to seek the necessary help or his objective inability to change, then he should seek laicization, be dismissed, or resign from ministry.

Canonical Loss of the Clerical State

In order to contextualize the option of resignation or removal from ministry, and to understand how the Church might react in cases of sexual abuse, it is critical to understand the Church's canonical norms and procedures regarding the loss of the clerical state itself.

The clerical state can be lost in one of two ways: (1) by the imposition of the penalty of dismissal initiated by a local ordinary, or (2) by a request for laicization initiated by the priest himself. Once dismissed, it is not normally possible for a cleric to return to ministry. On rare occasions, the Holy See will permit a laicized priest to return to ministry. However, this involves a lengthy period of rehabilitation.

The loss of the right to exercise priestly ministry occurs either through the imposition of a censure (also known as expiatory penalty), or by the declaration of an irregularity or impediment. These actions need not necessarily be perpetual in nature. If the problem is resolved, the penalty can be remitted or an irregularity or impediment dispensed, and the priest would be allowed to return to ministry.

Resigning from ministry is not intended to be an overwhelming or impossible process. Bishops are supposed to "assist in a fatherly way, 'in season and out of season,' priests who are facing a vocational crisis lest, in a matter of such great importance both for their own future and for the good of the church, they act precipitously and seek a dispensation without objectively serious reasons."[21]

Church law defines a priest in terms of three components: ordination, incardination, and faculties.

> *Ordination* is the sacrament of holy orders, a permanent configuration to the person of Christ. This permanence remains and can only be severed if the ordination itself is found invalid.

Incardination refers to the bond with a diocese or religious community in which priests exercise their ministry.

Faculties refer to the permission to perform priestly ministry. Some faculties are granted automatically upon ordination—for example, celebration of Mass, anointing the sick, and celebrating funeral rites—while others must be specifically given by the ordinary of the diocese, such as hearing confessions.

Once a priest has been granted faculties, he can usually exercise these anywhere in the world. Under certain circumstances, the bishop can revoke the faculties of a priest completely or partially, such as, for example, when permission to preach is suspended if homilies are considered offensive to church teaching(s). In addition, the bishop has the right to tell the superior of a religious community or institute to remove a priest from public ministry in a diocese.

It is also possible to remove all of a priest's faculties. In such cases, priests can no longer exercise their priestly ministry, and certain actions (for example, hearing confessions and presiding at marriages) would be invalid. Other actions, such as celebrating Mass publicly, would be considered valid but illicit, such as when the celebration of Mass is unauthorized.

By reason of ordination and incardination, the Church pledges to support priests financially by affording them a fitting remuneration. Normally, this remuneration consists of medical insurance, room and board, and a monthly stipend that varies among dioceses and/or depends on the priest's particular status. If a priest's faculties have been removed as the result of a canonical penalty or sanction, he is placed on administrative leave. His right to remuneration can be affected depending on the policies of his diocese or religious community. Only if a priest departs the clerical state by reason of laicization or the imposition of dismissal does he lose his right to remuneration. In these latter cases, the priest may be given financial severance.

Priests and deacons can approach their bishops by reason of incardination to request that a petition be sent to the Holy See asking for dispensation from all obligations arising from ordination, including celibacy. This process is referred to as a request for laicization. In danger of death or incidents of sexual misconduct, the only documentation required for laicization is the petition of the priest and the agreement of the bishop or religious superior.

In the case of serious actions, such as the sexual abuse of minors, the bishop or religious superior can initiate a penal process to seek dismissal from the clerical state. Canon law reserves penal cases to a collegiate tribunal of three judges, which can be expanded by the bishop to a panel of five if the case is more difficult. The Church considers a judicial penal process the normative manner for imposing the penalty of dismissal.

However, circumstances might arise that make it difficult, if not impossible, to make use of this judicial process. Two examples illustrate these problems. Intrinsic to the penal process is the question of prescription. Canon law provides for the possibility of imposing the penalty of dismissal in the case of a priest who "has committed an offense against the sixth commandment of the Decalogue, if the act was committed by force or threats or publicly or with a minor below the age of sixteen years."[22] Before 1994, such cases had to be prosecuted within a period of prescription of five years from the commission of the offense. Due to the large numbers of cases with lapsed prescription, the National Conference of Catholic Bishops was granted an extension of the period of prescription to ten years. Since April 25, 1994, the Church describes a minor as someone under the age of eighteen, and any sexual offenses against him or her can be prosecuted up to ten years after one's eighteenth birthday. Even with these expanded limits in place, a number of cases still come forward that are outside the period of prescription.

Extrinsic to the penal process is the problem of finding qualified personnel to conduct a penal process. Penal procedures are rare. They are undertaken only when all other means for dealing with a situation have failed. Diocesan tribunals do not conduct such trials on a regular basis. Their principal work is the examination of marriage cases. There are also significant procedural differences between a marriage and a penal case. The professionally trained canonical staffs of many tribunals are inadequate to deal with the requirements of a penal trial. A rural diocese, for example, may only have one or two qualified canonists who may only work part time in the tribunal. Other personnel may be serving as judges or defenders in marriage cases. Hence it becomes practically impossible for a diocese to form a tribunal for penal cases.

There are certainly ways of handling such difficulties. Qualified canonists can be brought in from outside the diocese and appointed to serve as ad hoc judges. This may avoid the difficult situation of priests passing judgment on other priests of the same region or diocese. It is also possible to approach the Apostolic Signatura of the Vatican and ask that a penal case be assigned to a larger tribunal with personnel capable of handling such matters. Unfortunately, even the Signatura is backlogged with marriage cases, so penal cases are not always possible.

In view of these difficulties, an administrative process, known as expiatory penalties, allows for dismissal from the clerical state by papal decree. This process is considered very controversial because it appears to deny a priest his basic right not to be punished with canonical penalties except according to the norm of civil law. It also compromises priests' right to self-defense. Despite its controversial nature, there remain good precedents for dismissing priests by papal decree. However, the process is used only as an exception and usually only occurs when priests refuse to request a dispensation from their clerical obligations following civil conviction.

Despite criticism that expiatory penalties seem overly punitive and inadequately pastoral, the Latin code maintains them, specifying some general principles regarding them and especially their effects. These penalties certainly envision the offender's spiritual well-being. However, more forcefully than censures, "expiatory" penalties emphasize remedying the social damage done by the delict and deterring others from similar behavior.[23]

The focus here is the social damage created by the serious misconduct of a priest who deeply wounds the victim, society, the Church, and himself. In the face of such a grave breach, it might well be expected that an offending priest receive a maximum penalty of dismissal from the clerical state. Although written in a different context, John Stuart Mill's distinction between self-regarding and other-regarding actions is applicable.

> [T]he individual is not accountable to society for his actions, insofar as these concern the interests of no person but himself" but "for such actions as are prejudicial to the interests of others, the individual is accountable, and may be subjected either to social or to legal punishment, if society is of [the] opinion that the one or the other is requisite for its protection.[24]

In light of these norms and procedures, a priest may depart the clerical state by way of laicization. He may also be dismissed by way of a tribunal or administrative decision. Another possible pastoral option may be resignation from ministry.

Canon 1044:2 provides a certain type of resignation for a priest whose behavior is such that he cannot or should not exercise priestly ministry. A priest can be removed from ministry when he is suffering from a psychological illness. Once the impediment is declared, the priest cannot exercise his priestly ministry until a cure is verified. In these cases, faculties and rights to remuneration remain, but there cannot be any exercise of ministry. The possibility remains for them to return to full or limited ministry.

The option of resignation from ministry, however, is also available to priests who cannot or do not desire to seek laicization or dismissal from the priesthood, but who realize that they have wounded the Church and society in some way. For them, resignation is a way to make amends and to preserve the Church from further harm. In such cases, priests take the initiative by asking their bishops to declare their impediment from the exercise of priestly ministry. This declaration, in effect, permits priests to resign. Priests who consider this option usually desire to remain priests despite their misconduct. The situation is not unlike that of divorced Catholics who do not seek annulments because they do not wish to have their marriage declared null, that is, as if it never existed. In other words, offending priests are amenable to rehabilitation but realize that their return to active ministry is simply not possible. They accept the fact that they have done harm. This option challenges the best instincts of priests regarding their own accountability.

This option respects the Church's law that we should not punish the sick but care for them. It also fosters the Church's compassion for the priest by allowing him to resign and offer this suffering for others.

Resigned priests cannot exercise their ministry in any way. They remain bound to all priestly obligations, as well as celibacy. While diocesan and religious communities have a responsibility to provide for their sustenance, resigned priests may be expected to pay for many—if not all—of their living needs. Stephen J. Rossetti has argued in "Priest Suicides and the Crisis of Faith" that priests who sexually molest children are often falsely considered "hopelessly damaged."[25] The option of resignation from ministry is not meant to foster this impression. Rather, resignation is meant to affirm that no one is beyond the healing power of God. No one is excluded from the path of recovery.

Repentance

Self-imposed or Church mandated penalties and limits on ministry must be understood within the context of repentance. Repentance is the sincere desire to change one's life at its core.[26] Repentance occurs in response to an awareness that one truly needs to change because to remain the same is egregiously unacceptable to oneself. Repentance arises as a result of seeing clearly, without distortion of the truth about oneself, with complete awareness of one's inadequacy, evil, selfishness, and sinfulness. True repentance has no room for excuses, defensiveness, or denial. True repentance takes full responsibility for one's actions and is willing to be stripped of pretensions in the service of being made better. Saint Peter's weeping after denying Christ is an eminent example of authentic repentance.

Protect and Heal

Ultimately, the bishops' *Charter*, *Essential Norms*, and the many actions that they have taken since their awareness of the extent of sexual abuse are meant to protect victims and promote healing. Many bishops have spoken and written apologies on behalf of priests who have abused children. They continue to reaffirm victims of their "zero tolerance" for abusive priests, deacons, and church personnel. They also continue to establish programs of spiritual, emotional, and social assistance. The bishops understand that victims of sexual abuse carry the trauma of their abuse for the rest of their lives, and thus there must be a network of ongoing support. The abuse remains a lasting mark of their seduction, but with the proper support, victims can renew their faith in the sacramental Church.

Important Distinctions

Newsweek's Kenneth L. Woodward states that a major problem now exists for the future of priestly vocations due to "the alliteration of priest and pedophile." Is this true? Are most cleric offenders pedophiles? Some recent surveys warn that the priesthood actually tends to attract more ephebophiles than pedophiles. What is the difference? Are they motivated by the same psychological and social factors?

In light of the variety of literature and opinions about the sexual-abuse crisis, it is important to clarify some terms.

> *Heterosexuals* possess a primary sexual desire toward persons of the opposite sex.

> *Homosexuals* possess a primary sexual desire toward persons of the same sex.

> *Bisexuals* possess a generally indiscriminate sexual desire to persons of both sexes.

Pedophiles possess a primary sexual desire for children between the ages of one and thirteen, with victims that are at least five years younger than perpetrators.

Ephebophiles possess a primary sexual desire for children between the ages of fourteen and seventeen, with victims that are at least five years younger than perpetrators.

Fixated offenders are only attracted to children, they often have no gender preference, they tend to cause the greatest physical harm (sometimes murder), and they almost always assault strangers. They represent about 15 percent of sexual offenders. Sexual desire for a fixated pedophile and ephebophile is intense and usually recurrent.

Fixated pedophiles and ephebophiles are developmentally arrested, psychosexually immature, nonassertive, often heterosexually inhibited, lacking in social skills, and without a basic knowledge of sexuality. They possess a need for control and children are perceived as compliant and manipulative. The fixated pedophile and ephebophile are at the same psychosexual age as the victim. Generally speaking, since fixated abusers target strangers, they usually do not seek out particular children. Rather, they are attracted to the sight, smell, and sound of virtually any child.

Power and control are critical factors. The child is yielding and vulnerable, perceived as unthreatening, unassertive, and lacking the ability to retaliate. In a sense, the fixated molester does what some adults choose to do with prostitutes—that is, they bypass personal autonomy.

Regressed offenders—often referred to as situational abusers—are usually people who under extreme stress regress to an impaired stage of development and act out by engaging in sex with children. Regressed pedophiles and ephebophiles usually appear to be very normal, sometimes going many years without acting out, and they do not always have a gender preference. They usually target children they know (for example, daughters, sons, nephews, students, and so forth). They account for about 85 percent of child molestation. Most clergy offenders are regressed offenders.

Regressed pedophiles and ephebophiles often play games with their victims, such as wrestling, tickling, or asking probing sexual questions of the victim. These pedophiles and ephebophiles often "court" their victim by games and manipulate them through invitations to movies, trips, and treats. Physical or emotional acting out stimulates the perpetrator and places a psychological distance between their feelings of loneliness and emptiness, and sexual excitement itself. Although pedophiles and ephebophiles often rationalize their molestation as helping the victim—for example, as caretaker, parent, teacher, or providing friendship—deviant sexual behavior is always an aggressive act, and the child is always a victim.

Causes for Sexual Abuse

The root causes for pedophilia and ephebophilia often vary, making it very difficult to stereotype the group. For example, sometimes sexual offenders are impaired by a homosexual desire that overrides their ability to differentiate the immorality of contact with adolescent—adultlike—youths. Psychologically, such attraction may be more homosexual than ephebophilic. Conversely, some sexual offenders are attracted to minors of the same sex, but their actions are motivated by psychological dysfunction instead of homosexual desire. Thus one must *not* conclude that all sexual offenders are homosexual.

No single explanation accounts for the different pathways that lead to pedophilia and ephebophilia. Any theory must be multifaceted and account for a wide range of behaviors, fantasies, and organic factors. A comprehensive theory of pedophilia and ephebophilia must refer to psychological, familial, environmental, social, genetic, hormonal, organic, and biological factors.

Clinical evaluations of pedophiles and ephebophiles reveal them to be a diverse group. They differ educationally, vocationally, religiously, and socioeconomically. They vary in the amount of force or aggression used in their sexual acts. They may be involved in a wide variety of other variant sexual behaviors, such as exhibitionism, voyeurism, frotteurism (sexually touching or fondling an unwilling person), masochism, sadism, and so forth.

There are several theories that attempt to capture the root causes of child abuse, and they are helpful for understanding the range of possibilities for clergy abuse.

Psychoanalytic theories look at deviant sexual behavior as stemming from early childhood trauma during ages two to five. Sexual or physical abuse leaves the child in a state of overstimulation, confusion, and rage. Feeling helpless and powerless, this victim may sexually act out as a way of re-creating the original trauma, hoping to overcome the anxiety associated with it. This victim may also identify with the abusing adult and act out sexually with a younger child. Acting out makes the adult feel alive and vital, and reestablishes a feeling of control and power. This feeling of dominance soon dissipates, however, and the reenactment is repeated, forcing the individual to molest over and over again.

Family system theories stress the role of unresolved inter-generational family dynamics on specific family members. This occurs when an unconscious conflict is encouraged in a child. For example, the system fails when parents have children to satisfy their own unconscious need for love or attention. Such parents expect unrealistic levels of obedience and, as a result, children spend their lives searching for their own, hidden destiny. The children may spend their entire life searching for something they lost—or were denied—in childhood.

Behaviorism and social learning theories stress the fact that sexual pleasure reinforces behavior. A child who has been assaulted by an adult or other child feels guilt associated with the sexual pleasure. When these victims become adults, they experience internal conflict and ambivalence that sometimes motivates them to act out sexually with children.

Biological theories stress the possibility of brain illness or damage as a cause of deviant sexual arousal. These studies have uncovered a variety of causes. For example, too much of the male hormone testosterone has been known to cause violence and chaotic sexual behavior, precipitated, for instance, by a mother's stress during pregnancy, the intake of specific drugs, or the presence of brain abnormalities that create specific behavioral problems.

Personality Dysfunctions

Regardless of the root causes of sexual abuse, pedophiles and ephebophiles (fixated or regressed) display four personality dysfunctions that can serve as indicators of possible danger. Through psychological surveys, sexual history profiles, and interviews, formation teams should be able to identify seminarians and priests that tend to struggle with the following personality issues:

Emotional congruence: children have a special meaning because of their lack of dominance and power.

Sexual arousal: children are the object of sexual stimulation due to specific characteristics. For example, some prefer boys that lack pubic hair or girls that are blonde and blue-eyed.

Blockage: pedophiles and ephebophiles have no capacity for authentic heterosexual or homosexual relationships.

Disinhibition: pedophiles and ephebophiles often use alcohol or other drugs to lower inhibitions prior to the sexual acting out with children.

Narcissism

Narcissism is another personality trait that is worthy of special attention for seminarians and priests. According to Paul Duckro and Marc Falkenhain, "narcissism sets the stage for clergy sexual abuse."[27] Narcissism is an attitude of entitlement that may manifest itself as a personality disorder. It is a pervasive pattern of grandiosity, need for admiration, and lack of empathy. This sense of entitlement permits a narcissist to operate outside the limits and rules of societal groups.[28] This sense of entitlement is dangerous as it leads to extensive and self-convincing rationalizations of very dangerous, immoral, and criminal behavior. It also leads to a sense of "never enough," which is an indicator of addiction.

Narcissists do not understand the impact of the hurt and trauma that they cause. They normally have low self-esteem, with no empathy for others. Most narcissists fall into one of two categories: (1) Covert narcissists feel superior and special, but also vulnerable and cautious. They carry a lot of inner pain and might be open to change. (2) Overt narcissists must hit rock bottom by running into some catastrophic experience before any change in behavior can be considered necessary. In either case, the excessive focus on oneself prevents empathy from forming and easily leads the narcissist into the dark realm of sexual abuse of minors.

Cybersex or Internet Sex Addiction

Today's understanding of addiction goes well beyond former generations that focused solely on the misuse of alcohol and other drugs. We are now aware of the aimless search for wholeness and happiness that manifests itself in a variety of addictive behaviors, such as eating, working, gambling, shopping, stealing, and the Internet. At its most basic level, an addiction is an attempt to control what the addict feels powerless to resist. Therefore, addictive behavior creates a vicious cycle that leads to further out-of-control activity and powerlessness.[29]

Three criteria serve as indicators for addictive behavior. *Com-*

pulsivity is the loss of ability to choose freely whether to stop or to continue. *Continuation* drives the addictive behavior despite adverse consequences. *Obsession* is a preoccupation that focuses exclusively on a particular behavior.

By its very nature, addiction affects one both psychologically and spiritually. It is truly a "soul sickness."[30] Addiction comes from the Latin word *addicere*, "to give up, surrender, or dedicate one's service to another." Essentially, it means to deliver oneself to a master. Addiction is "fundamentally a misdirected spiritual search that is rooted in a fundamental belief that I am not OK the way I am and there is a void that needs to be filled and something external to myself will fill this void."[31]

Addictive behavior provides a temporary sense of relief and the feeling of control. In spiritual terms, addiction attempts to replace God with objects or attachments that command allegiance. As such, Alcoholics Anonymous rightly identifies addiction as a form of spiritual bankruptcy.[32] It is the temporary escape from the real dilemmas of the empty soul. Addicts wish to avoid the inner feelings of unworthiness and instead engage in a spiraling cycle of preoccupation. This may also lead them into exhibiting a double life, whereby they act one way in public and another in private in order to fulfill their urgent desire to hide the truth. At their core, most addicts are truly frightened to think of what life would be like without the addictive behavior. They reject that human wholeness is a matter of accepting one's strengths *and* limitations.[33] "No one can be at home in his own heaven until he has learned to be at home in his own hell."[34] In other words, everyone must come to terms with his or her own weaknesses, limitations, and sinfulness.

Patrick Carnes describes the pattern of sexual compulsivity as a cycle of preoccupation with sexual thoughts and fantasies that lead to ritualized behaviors.[35] The cycle manifests itself on four levels: preoccupation, ritualization, compulsive sexual behavior, and despair. The cycle that leads to sexual compulsion may appear innocent enough at first, like checking one's email. If there is no e-mail, the addict spirals down a path of compulsive behavior, checking their e-mail again and again, each time without a response.[36] Each repetition of the ritual increases their level of despair and eventually the addict satisfies their desire by acting out sexually. For them, sex is the strongest way to alleviate their increasing sense of unworthiness. In other words, sex temporarily thwarts the endless feeling that their needs will never be truly met.[37] Unfortunately, however, the sexual act only serves to exasperate their thoughts and fantasies, and it makes them more vulnerable to simple triggers (such as checking e-mail) and ends in deeper despair.

Cybersex, or sex via the Internet, is sparked by an obsession with finding one image, conversation, or person who holds the key to happiness and fulfillment.[38] Hours often pass during the attempt to find "perfect sex" on the Internet. The pursuit is illusive since the Internet feeds fantasy and not reality. The Internet fosters pseudo-relationships that can be terminated with a click of the mouse.

Cybersex Tools

Clergy with cybersex problems tend to be younger, they average twelve hours per week online, and they have many different ways of satisfying their desire on the Internet:[39]

Online Search Engines: Internet browsers such as Netscape, Internet Explorer, and Opera, for example, allow users to find Web pages that may contain pornographic texts, sounds, and images.

Newsgroups: Online bulletin boards or forums dedicated to specific topics where users can post and read texts or multimedia messages, such as pictures, sounds, and video.

E-mail: Browser-based Internet mail (for example, Yahoo Mail or Microsoft Hotmail) or special mail software (for example, Microsoft Outlook) can be used for direct communication with other individuals.

Chat Rooms: Text-based virtual meeting places for real-time conversation with anyone logged into the system. Both sexualized conversation and multimedia can be exchanged in chat rooms. Popular chat rooms include Yahoo Chat or America Online Chat. Most chat areas have sections dedicated to sexual chats (one of the largest is Internet Relay Chat [IRC]). Some have chat rooms specifically dedicated to the exchange of pornography through file servers (virtual warehouses that store information).

Videoconferencing: The Internet is used for "live" cybersex sessions containing real-time video and instant still images.

Telephony Software: Allows users to send and receive phone calls over the Internet at a very low cost. Rates are the same for any call throughout the world.

Peer-to-Peer File Sharing: These software applications allow users to share personal files (directly from computer to computer) with any other users that are logged into the system. Napster and Kazaa, for example, are two organizations that offer software packages that allow users to search and access pornographic files. One study reported that 42 percent of all Kazaa requests were for either adult or child pornography.[40]

Online Gaming: Many gaming software packages include direct links to virtual reality environments that foster synchronous communication between persons and allow for creative building of virtual spaces. In other words, gamers can create their own characters and act out their fantasies in a virtual setting. Unfortunately, many game programs are sexually charged and, therefore, they can tend to trigger sexually deviant behavior.

Types of Cybersex Addicts

In cybersex use, three types of groups can be noted. There is the "discovery group" who never had any problems with sexual fantasy or behavior until they discovered sex on the Internet. This discovery fosters the development of compulsive behavior. The "predisposed group" is made up of individuals who have had some history of problematic sexual thoughts and fantasies. Here the Internet fosters the development of already existing sexual desires. Finally, there is the "lifelong sexually compulsive group" who have been involved in sexually compulsive behavior for a long time. The Internet simply becomes an additional way of acting out their inappropriate sexual behaviors. Some in this group might feel that cybersex offers them a "safer" place to act out, rather than in direct contact with others.

Researchers suggest several reasons for cybersex activity.[41] It is everywhere and impossible to avoid. It has public availability with an endless supply of sexual materials. It is inexpensive. It is isolating, yet interactive, and becomes intoxicating.

Certain predisposing problems make some clergy vulnerable to sexually addictive behaviors. For example, some seek priesthood as a way of escaping shame. For others, it feeds an excessive need for affirmation. Some have had sexual issues for many years and they are living in denial. Still, others are predisposed with a great deal of unexpressed anger or they perceive themselves as bad or unworthy. In such cases, clergy might become sexually addictive to take care of their emotional needs.

What Can the Church Do About Cybersex?

What can seminaries, houses of formation, presbyterates, and religious communities do to discourage cybersex? First, there must be a willingness to speak about sexual issues in an appropriate setting. Applicants to seminaries and houses of formation must be asked such questions as "Do you intentionally visit sexual sites on the Internet?" "Do you use online chat rooms as a way to relieve feelings of isolation and loneliness?" Second, seminaries, houses of formation, dioceses, and religious communities must facilitate workshops on the moral and ethical use of the Internet and should develop acceptable use policies.

In its document *The Church and the Internet,* the Pontifical Council for Social Communications advises that "education and training regarding the Internet ought to be part of a comprehensive program of media education available to members of the Church. As much as possible, pastoral planning for social communications should make provision for this training in the formation of seminarians, priests, religious, and lay pastoral personnel as well as teachers, parents, and students."[42] The pontifical council interprets cyberspace—and by association, cybersex—as a new disorder that they define as Internet Addiction.[43]

Particularly dangerous for the sex addict is the progression from initial inquisitiveness to an unmanageable preoccupation with discovering new and more stimulating forms of erotic material. For some, this can spiral toward acting out (for example, masturbation or sex with others). Those with a deeply ingrained sex addiction often try to convince themselves that they can control their addictive behavior by a supreme effort of the will and by a deep commitment to spirituality. Personal control and prayer are seen as the tools for outwitting their cunning and powerful compulsion.[44] Patrick Carnes notes that a sex addict may act out of several planes:[45]

1. Masturbation, compulsive sexual activity, pornography, and prostitution
2. Exhibitionism, voyeurism, indecent phone calls, and indecent liberties
3. Child molestation, incest, or rape

Carnes argues that it is not unusual for a sex addict to progress from one level to the next as the need grows. "From masturbation to voyeurism to cruising is not a long journey."[46] Until the sex addict admits that the problem is within and not "out there," recovery cannot begin. There are no half-measures for the addict.[47]

Cybersex Test

Kimberly Young offers a helpful test to examine Internet use. She considers an affirmative response to five or more of the following questions as qualifying someone as addicted.[48]

1. Do you feel preoccupied with the Internet?
2. Do you feel the need to use the Internet with increasing amounts of time in order to achieve satisfaction?
3. Have you repeatedly made unsuccessful efforts to control, cut back, or stop Internet use?
4. Do you feel restless, moody, depressed, or irritable when attempting to cut down or stop Internet use?
5. Do you stay online longer than originally intended?
6. Have you jeopardized or risked the loss of a significant relationship, job, educational, or career opportunity because of the Internet?
7. Have you lied to family members, therapists, or others to conceal the extent of involvement with the Internet?
8. Do you use the Internet as a way of escaping from problems or of relieving a dysphoric mood (for example, feelings of helplessness, guilt, anxiety, or depression)?

Many people frequently live with addictions without recognizing them. Just like a chronic, debilitating disease or disorder that will only grow worse, Internet addiction and cybersex are systemic ways of estranging and alienating one's self from God and others. Seminary, diocesan, and religious personnel must offer comprehensive ethical programs on the proper and improper use of the internet.[49]

Accountability for Sexual Formation

We must never forget that the candidate [for the diocesan or religious priesthood] himself is a necessary and irreplaceable agent in his own formation. All formation is ultimately a self-formation. No one can replace us in the responsible freedom that we have as individual persons. The future priest "must grow in his awareness that the agent *par excellence* of his formation is the Holy Spirit, who by the gift of a new heart configures and conforms him to Jesus Christ the good shepherd.[50]

[Priests must] carry out a permanent formation which will respond appropriately to the greatness of God's gift and to the urgency of the demands and requirement of our time....[E]ach priest has the duty, rooted in the sacrament of holy orders, to be faithful to the gift God has given him and to respond to the call for daily conversion which comes with the gift itself.[51]

Priest-psychiatrist James J. Gill, SJ, and others affirmed that seminaries must strengthen entrance requirements and put into place ongoing formational programs for assisting seminarians to cope with their sexuality. As explored in the previous chapter, taking a sexual history can be an integral part of these requirements. Seminaries and houses of formation need to create an atmosphere where seminarians are comfortable talking about their sexuality to spiritual directors and mentors, especially strengthened if the seminary has on staff a person learned in the study of sexuality. However, formation must remain the central focus and responsibility of every individual. The Church can provide tools for formation, but it cannot force development.

Pope John XXIII chose as his motto *Obedientia et pax*. Peace comes from knowing oneself as given over and entrusted to the will of God. Among many other things, this self-knowing demands a rigorous honesty regarding one's sexual health and integrity. Calm will not occur until everything possible is done to prevent sexual disorder among priests.

7

Celibacy
"Radical Discipleship"

Seminarians and priests are called to give wholehearted witness to their ministry by living celibately. Their primary task is not simply caring for those in need, for all kinds of people can offer devoted service. Nor is it counseling, for many able professionals do this. Nor is it church management, for managers abound. Our fundamental responsibility is to proclaim the gospel and celebrate the sacraments as celibate men.

The third edition of the *Program of Priestly Formation* states that "the celibate commitment remains one of the most fundamental expressions of Jesus' call to radical discipleship for the sake of the Kingdom. From a Christian point of view, there is no more positive, stronger witness to the kingdom than a willingness to live without wife and family as Jesus did."[1] This type of discipleship demands that a person takes on the likeness of Jesus Christ and this "taking on" enables the priest to live the celibate life meaningfully.

Pastores Dabo Vobis indicates that celibacy demands a "mature and free decision…built on esteem for priestly friendship and self-discipline, as well as on the acceptance of solitude and on a physically and psychologically sound personal state."[2] Canon law spells out these demands. To live celibately means to observe perfect and perpetual continence, for the sake of the kingdom, as a special gift from God, by which ministers can more easily adhere to Christ with an undivided heart, and can more freely dedicate themselves to the service of God and humankind.[3]

Biblical Testimony

Celibacy is the voluntary foregoing of a marital relationship and the genital expression of one's sexual identity for the sake of God and the Church. The biblical testimony about celibacy provides a helpful and instructive path into the deep meaning of celibacy. In Matthew 19:3–13, Jesus is confronted by some Pharisees about the question of divorce. Jesus answers that no human must separate what God has joined together. His disciples respond that it is "better not to marry." Jesus instructs them that not everyone can accept this message but "only those to whom it is given." Jesus further explains that some people are incapable of marriage, while "some have renounced marriage for the sake of the kingdom of heaven." The words of Jesus indicate that there are some who are able to forego marriage and genital relationships for a higher purpose, the kingdom of God.[4] Jesus does not denigrate sexuality or marriage; he upholds the fact that the decision not to marry is a free choice and a gift. "Not all can accept this word, but only those to whom that is granted."

In 1 Corinthians 7:1–15, Paul also addresses the question of marriage and divorce. Paul writes that "I wish that all were as I myself am….To the unmarried and the widows I say that it is well for them to remain unmarried as I am. But if they are not practicing self-control, they should marry" (6–9). Paul sees celibacy and marriage as separate but different ways of life, both gifts from God. Paul is not exhorting people to celibacy, but rather to see it as a valued gift from God that is given to some.

The biblical testimony about celibacy raises significant points of reflection. First, Jesus himself was celibate. His life was entirely devoted to God. Second, celibacy is well-suited for some because it assists them to devote themselves to God and to the proclamation of the gospel. Third, because celibacy is suited only to some, it will always be restricted. It is a special gift that calls for a free acceptance. Fourth, celibacy must be linked to prayer in order to develop a closeness to God. Celibacy can flourish only in a person who is utterly devoted to God and the Church. Celibacy is intended to call one to a more transcendent awareness that there is much more to life than we experience here and now.

Receiving and Appropriating the Gift

One of the gifts of the Church is "reception" (to take in, accept, adopt), "a process whereby the faithful accept a teaching or decision of the Church" and affirm a teaching or practice "through steady observance."[5] Anyone desiring to live celibately must receive and appropriate this gift through steady and resolute self-giving.

In its 1974 document *A Guide to Formation in Priestly Celibacy*, the Congregation for Catholic Education summarizes the Church's embrace of the gift of celibacy:

> Celibacy, which is a value, a grace, a charism, has to be presented in its true light if it is to be appreciated, chosen, and genuinely lived. Its presentation, therefore, must be calm and serene, confronting the prejudices and objections currently brought against it. . [.Voluntary celibacy makes sense when it is viewed in a context of relationships with others lived in a fraternal community where one can "reach" others without "having" them, i.e., when it is an exercise in nonpossessiveness.] It is a sign of celibacy rightly assumed when one can create and maintain worthwhile interpersonal relationships while experiencing the presence of friends even in their absence, refusing to impose oneself on them…[I]t can be said that celibacy is also an acceptance of "solitude."[6]

Fraternal Life

A Guide to Formation in Priestly Celibacy teaches that celibacy demands a progressive development of one's sexual and emotional powers, a selfless openness to affection, and a deep friendship with Christ that extends to everyone without exception.[7] Following the direction of the 1990 Synod of Bishops, *Pastores Dabo Vobis* outlines certain criteria for proper "education in celibacy." A bishop must show concern and share fraternal life with his priests. There must be a proper development of the psychological and sexual maturity of seminarians and priests. They need to develop an assiduous and authentic life of prayer, with active access to a spiritual director. Acceptance of priestly friendship and self-discipline is critical, along with an acceptance of solitude.[8]

In order to achieve these goals, it is important that a seminary, diocese, or religious community supports a "celibate community," a fraternity where everyone is honestly committed to living out the demands of chaste celibacy. This community climate encourages and gives good example to others. It also serves as a corrective when breaches of celibacy are known or detected. Living celibately is not primarily a matter of control. It is a matter of where one's heart is anchored. A strong and passionate love for Jesus and the priesthood is the necessary guarantee of remaining true to a life of celibacy.

Necessities of Celibacy

A deep love for Christ entails a personal appropriation of Jesus' own celibacy.[9] Jesus' intimacy with God and his preaching of the kingdom are all-consuming. As he transcends the limits of a single family, "he does so to give himself ever more fully to his Father in heaven and his family of believers on earth, and there is no departure from this single-minded dedication."[10] For the sake of the kingdom of heaven, Jesus raises celibacy as a special gift for some disciples, a charism that exceeds what the world deems possible (Matthew 19:10–12). In the commitment to celibacy, priests "promise to bestow on the people they serve the love, affection, and devotion they would have given to a natural family. They are called 'father' and regard those they serve as 'brothers' and 'sisters.'"[11] The celibate commitment transcends the human powers of any person. It rests only on the power of God to enable a priest to give up a natural family for a family of faith.

Celibacy is not in vogue in our contemporary culture. It does not receive wholehearted support. Before committing to a celibate lifestyle, then, an individual must carefully discern whether or not God is offering this gift *and* whether or not they have the capacity to live out the gift authentically.[12] Are personal will and abilities in tune with the will of God? Three levels of discernment are necessary to determine the appropriateness of celibacy. Do I love my own incarnation by an authentic appropriation of my sexuality? Do I see myself as a unity of body and soul, aware of my affectivity and needs? Do I deeply know and accept the fact that God loves me and calls me only to be what is the very best for me? A commitment to celibacy comes only after this discernment.

The Basic Plan for the Ongoing Formation of Priests insists that the spiritual formation of priests is shaped decisively by their celibate commitment.[13] Only an individual's unity with Jesus makes the celibate commitment possible. The seminary lays an important framework for celibate living, but only ongoing formation *in* celibacy makes this commitment strong enough to face questions and challenges. Ongoing formation in celibacy entails living comfortably with the renunciation of genital sex and marriage. This necessitates an honest facing of one's sexuality. The overall aim of celibacy is deepening the experiences of solitude, communion, love, and giving life. Its motivation is pastoral charity. Formation in celibacy demands three necessities.

The rationale for celibacy: Seminarians and priests need to consistently revisit and reappropriate the meaning of celibacy in their lives. Husbands and wives cannot take each other for granted. Seminarians and priests, too, cannot take celibacy for granted. It is necessary to review and reclaim one's commitment to celibacy.

The celibate portrait: It is important to learn and constantly refine the human, interpersonal, and spiritual strategies for healthy and generative loving and living. A key component is accountability to self and others (at least with one other trusted confidant). Just as infidelity corrodes a marriage, infidelity corrodes celibacy. Priests must honestly face and deal with the temptations they may experience regarding their celibate commitment.[14]

The qualities of contemplation, gratitude, vulnerability and generosity are critical for living authentic celibacy.[15] When these qualities coalesce in an individual's heart, celibacy assumes a compelling attractiveness in a life of distinctive service for God and the Church. Authentic celibate living should be differentiated from bachelor living, particularly the type that endorses a superior, detached, critical attitude. Celibate life likewise does not mean the life of a workaholic, compulsively searching for work and other things. True celibate priests should also shun any urges toward clericalism, the unfounded sense of superiority, expecting exaggerated signs of respect and privilege.

Supportive resources: Seminarians and priests need personal, social, and ecclesial resources that nourish and support their celibacy. "With a reason, with means, and with support, celibacy is not only tolerable but indeed a fulfilling path of loving God and others and bringing new life to the world."[16]

Celibacy vs. Chastity

The terms *chastity* and *celibacy* are often used interchangeably. Recent Church documents often use the term *celibate chastity*. It is important to see these terms in their separateness to better value their connectedness. Celibacy is a free choice or promise to perfectly and perpetually live a single, chaste life.

In the 1991 document *Human Sexuality: A Catholic Perspective for Education and Lifelong Learning*, the U.S. bishops define chastity as a way of "guiding the sexual instinct to the service of love and of integrating it in the development of the person....Chastity truly consists in the long-term integration of one's thoughts, feelings, and actions in a way that values, esteems, and respects the dignity of oneself and others. Chastity frees us from the tendency to act in a manipulative or exploitative manner in our relationships and enables us to show true love and kindness always."[17]

The *Catechism of the Catholic Church* summarizes the Church's teaching in this fashion:

> Chastity means the successful integration of sexuality within the person and thus the inner unity of man in his bodily and spiritual being. Sexuality, in which man's belonging to the bodily and biological world is expressed, becomes personal and truly human when it is integrated into the relationship of one person to another, in the complete and lifelong mutual gift of a man and a woman.
>
> The virtue of chastity therefore involves the integrity of the person and the integrality of the gift.[18]

Chastity is a "vocation." It does not tolerate a double or duplicitous life. It includes an apprenticeship in self-mastery, aware that only gradually do we learn to rid ourselves of slavery to passion and reach the goal of freely choosing what is good and true. As such, chastity sustains growth that progresses in stages, despite human imperfection and sin. It is a deeply personal task rooted in baptism and blossoming in friendship.[19] Chastity must be situated in its baptismal context and within an integrated sexual integrity.[20]

Chastity places different demands on different vocations (for example, single, marriage, and religious or consecrated life). What is acceptable for the single vocation, such as dating and certain expressions of intimacy, would be inappropriate for consecrated life. Some behaviors appropriate in marriage, for example, genital intimacy, would be inappropriate for single life. For one committed to celibate chastity, engagement in genital sex is a violation of the sixth and ninth commandments, as well as a breach of one's promise or vow.[21] Should this violation be with a minor, one also commits a criminal act.

Chastity is not primarily about the suppression of desire.[22] Desire and the passions contain deep truths about who we are and what we need. Suppression of desire makes a person spiritually dead. We must educate our desires to see what they truly want and liberate them from small and insignificant pleasures. Saint Thomas Aquinas taught that being chaste is to live "in accordance with the truth of things."[23] Passion and desire can drive one into fantasy. Chastity brings us down to earth.[24]

The grace and exercise of chastity is particularly challenging with respect to fantasies such as infatuation and lust. Infatuation and lust are mirror images of each other. One often accompanies the other. With infatuation, there may be the temptation to think that another person is everything, all that we seek, the fulfillment of our longings.[25] Lust, on the other hand, is an attraction that disregards the humanity of others. Those who lust objectify their desire, ignoring human needs and identity. Aquinas notes that lust devours chastity in the same way as the lion sees the stag only as a meal. Lust damages chastity as it seeks to entrap others. Lust is an impulse to take control and make ourselves God. Lust is "sexual passion as a cover-story for the will of God....The task before us is not to subject sexual passion to the will, but to restore it to desire, whose origin and end is God, whose liberation is God's grace made manifest in the life, teaching, crucifixion and resurrection of Jesus Christ."[26]

Solitude

Every individual retains a solitude that cannot be abolished. Rainer Maria Rilke captures the importance of solitude in one's vocation.

> A good marriage is that in which each appoints the other guardian of his solitude, and shows him this confidence, the greatest in his power to bestow....Once the realization is accepted that even between the closest human beings infinite distances continue to exist, a wonderful living side by side can grow up, if they succeed in loving the distance between them which makes it possible for each to see the other whole and against a wide sky."[27]

The life of a celibate seminarian or priest is also rooted in solitude. Jean Vanier has noted that "loneliness is part of being human because there is nothing in existence that can completely fulfill the needs of the human heart."[28] Recognizing our uniqueness, we can be empowered by solitude as we seek to understand the origin of our desires and direct them toward the proper end—God.

The Call to Celibacy

Celibacy is a vocation given as a gift. The one called to be celibate is enabled to do so by grace.[29] Celibacy is a call that develops from within. It emerges slowly and often falters along the way. A priest becomes a "celibate at heart" when he experiences an existential inability to become himself in any lifestyle except celibacy. It takes time for this deep discernment to occur, which is a basic reason why men should not be accepted into formation programs until they have lived celibately for some time. If God has ignited the flame, the fire will persist.

A healthy celibate is physically healthy and enjoys what he is doing. He is aware of boundaries by respecting others. He is able to endure sacrifice and suffering and empowering others, while maintaining a sense of his own identity. He has positive friendships with women and men. He is able to balance time alone and with others. He possesses a good sense of humor. He is spiritually balanced, self-confident, and generous.[30]

These qualities do not come easily or automatically. They emerge from prayer, reflection, and maturity. As Dorothy Day wrote in *The Long Loneliness*, "All my life I have been haunted by God....I do not remember that I was articulate or reasoned about this love, but it warmed and filled my heart."[31]

Letting Go and Finding Joy

In the process of allowing oneself to be inflamed by God's gift of celibacy, it is essential for a priest to acknowledge what he is leaving behind. Dorothy Day spoke of a "willing celibate" as one who embraces a celibate vocation and remains joyful and peaceful, who knows the long loneliness and properly sets out on the journey of grieving.

Seminarians and priests committed to celibacy must grieve by acknowledging what they are renouncing. There are important steps in this grieving process: acknowledge the reality of the loss, identify and express emotions of grief, commemorate the loss (for example, at simple or final vows), acknowledge conflicting emotions, resolve these ambivalences, let go, and move on. Joyce Rupp, OSM, warns of the dangers of not grieving:

> All of us have those turns in the road. It is what we do or do not do with them that make the difference. All too often we can let a difficult life transition sit in our soul, discomforting us, empty us, discourage us and sometimes strangle us with its strong clenching hold....It keeps raising its voice inside us, at times when we least expect it. It drowns out the voice of joy in our life, bleeds our spirit of energy and enthusiasm; it destroys belief in the ability to rise from the ashes of our pain.[32]

Seminarians and priests must not let the pangs of celibacy drown the voice of joy. For those called to the life of celibacy, overcoming grief should lead to comfort, fulfillment, and encouragement.

Authentic Celibacy

Seminarians and priests find a reason within themselves to live celibacy authentically. Not everyone can accept celibacy (Matthew 19:11). It has its origins in a divine donation. A priest must accept and embrace celibacy wholeheartedly and with purity of heart. "The Church sees a sign of the priest's special consecration to Christ as one who has left everything to follow him."[33] Celibate priests affirms what Peter spoke to Jesus, "We have left everything and followed you" (Matthew 19:27, Mark 10:28, and Luke 18:28).

The purpose of celibacy in Matthew is "for the sake of the kingdom of heaven" (19:12) and for Paul it is to be "anxious about the affairs of the Lord, how to please the Lord" (1 Corinthians 7:32). In both cases the center of one's life revolves around God.

Conclusion

After God disclosed to Moses that the Lord is "a God merciful and gracious, / slow to anger, / and abounding in steadfast love and faithfulness, / keeping steadfast love for the thousandth generation, / forgiving iniquity and transgression and sin…," Moses bowed down to the ground in worship and asked a favor, "O Lord, I pray, let the Lord go with us" (Exodus 34:6–9).

Seminarians and priests need to make Moses' invitation their own, "…do come along in our company." In his keynote address to the Serra Club in 2004, Archbishop William J. Levada of San Francisco made reference to the recently publicized failings of some priests and bishops, a sad reality that has tarnished the reputation of the Catholic clergy in general. Archbishop Levada described these events as a time of "a great purification" in the Church as a priestly vocation can no longer be understood as "a path to prestige." He recalls the description of the first disciples by Saint John Chrysostom, "They were fearful, timid men, the evangelists make clear….What did they say of them? That when Christ was arrested, the others fled, despite all the miracles they had seen, while he who was the leader of the others denied him!"[1]

The New Testament demonstrates that Jesus did not call men who were saints. He did call them to become saints. Today's priestly vocations follow an identical path. This road is not a call to mediocrity. It is not an acceptance of the lowest common denominator. A priestly calling is twofold: a true recognition of one's fragile humanity and a deeply accepted acknowledgment that one is called to a life of holiness. Jesus did not permit Peter to feed his lambs and tend his sheep until Peter said three times that he loved him (see John 21:15–19).

Peter and all subsequent ministers in the Church cannot hear Jesus' request to "follow him" until after one honestly and deeply avows love of the Lord. No one has the right to do ministry until they have first pledged, over and over again, their love of the Lord. It is this love that gradually transforms timidity into ability, and weakness into strength.

Thérèse of Lisieux suggested that as humans we are "exiles of the heart." We must overcome this condition through mysticism, by spiritual communion with Jesus and one another in charity, patience, goodness, long-suffering, faith, fidelity, mildness, and chastity.[2] Short-circuiting love of Jesus and a mystical life is like trying to write a masterpiece overnight.

Human formation depends on an intense and personal holiness of life. This demands that seminarians and priests embody the virtues of courage, fortitude, and perseverance.[3] Spiritual leadership is not a job or career for the moment, but a lifelong vocation.

This spiritual vocation calls for a vision that announces God's interest for human beings, the world, and the Church. This vision demands that seminarians and priests have the capacity to preach the kingdom of God as all-inclusive, discern how God is acting in the world and the Church, honor the reality that God's kingdom gives privilege to the least, and understand that the kingdom of God is already present, but not yet fully realized. A priest's heart is exposed through his grasp of this vision.

A spiritual leader must want what God wants. Saint Augustine states:

> I must distinguish carefully between two aspects of the role the Lord has given me, a role that demands a rigorous accountability, a role based on the Lord's greatness rather than on my own merit. The first aspect is that I am a Christian; the second, that I am a leader. I am a Christian for my own sake, whereas I am a leader for your sake; the fact that I am a Christian is to my own advantage, but I am a leader for your advantage.[4]

The spirituality of a priest must exhibit a peacefulness of heart. It must demonstrate a pervasive compassion and a martyr's strength: God, grant me serenity to accept the things I cannot change, courage to change the things I can, and wisdom to know the difference. I must live one day at a time, accepting hardship as a pathway to peace; taking, as Jesus did, this sinful world as it is, not as I would have it; trusting that you, Lord, will make all things right if I surrender to your will so that I may be reasonably happy in this life and supremely happy with you forever in the next.[5]

Recent impressions of the priesthood often assume that it is dysfunctional and that priests are particularly prone to human and sexual problems. Some maintain that priests are poorly prepared and that they live in unhealthy, sexually stunted clerical environments.[6] Between September 2003 and January 2004, a survey of diocesan and religious priests was taken in eleven dioceses, with 64 percent of the priests responding. The survey revealed that happiness and satisfaction in the priestly ministry were strong and consistent, with 88 percent of these priests saying that they would choose priesthood again.

In 2002, a *Los Angles Times* survey showed that 91 percent of 1,854 priests surveyed were satisfied with the "way their lives as priests are going these days." Ninety percent said they would do it all over again. According to this survey, 90 percent of the priests responding spoke of the "joy of administering the sacraments and presiding at liturgy," "satisfaction of preaching the Word," and "the opportunity to work with many people and be part of their lives."[7] Despite the clergy sexual-abuse crisis, 84 percent of priests said that they are "proud to be a priest today."[8] Priests worry about accusations that might be brought against them. Some felt that they are "one phone call away from the rest of their lives being over." When asked if they were happy with their ministry, 90 percent replied affirmatively, with the same percentage saying that they are "committed to the ministry of the Catholic Church." Ninety-five percent professed to a "personal relationship with Jesus that is nourishing." Stephen J. Rossetti comments, "We are blessed to have such strong men of faith serving the people of God."[9]

There are not two journeys for every person, one spiritual and the other human. There is only one journey that encompasses both spiritual and human dimensions. The Gerasene demoniac in Mark 5:1–20 is an example. The man was possessed by legions of demons. He had lost his humanity. He lived among the dead in the tombs. He was distant from the human community. He was alone, naked, and he never rested. Day and night he screamed and gashed himself with stones. He had no inner tranquillity or center and was tortured by his rage.[10] His violence was directed inward, but possessed the possibility of hurting others. His behavior was self-destructive. He lived in isolation and inner torture.[11]

After his meeting with Jesus, witnesses "caught sight of him… sitting there clothed and in his right mind." The man had become humanly and spiritually whole. Spiritual and human wholeness go hand in hand. Only when the finite and the infinite meet can we transcend the fragilities of our humanity. The human and the spiritual dimensions of one's life are two sides of the same coin.

In 1792 John Carroll, the first bishop of the United States, wrote:

> It is notorious to you all that the present clergymen are insufficient for the exigencies of the faithful; and that they will be more and more so as the population of our county increases too rapidly. Unless, by providence of our good and merciful God, a constant supply of zealous and able pastors can be formed amongst ourselves.[12]

The number of Catholics in the United States is now over sixty-seven million. Archbishop Carroll's concern remains our concern. We must all work for greater numbers of zealous and able priests.

Appendix One
Code of Ethics

Statement of Commitment

At the beginning of each year, after proper explanation and motivation, every seminarian should be required to sign and live by a "Statement of Commitment to Community and Behavioral Standards":

1. I acknowledge at all times that I am in priestly formation and my behavior must reflect this fact.
2. I am the primary agent of my own spiritual, moral, intellectual, and psychological growth. Both the seminary as a house of formation, and the community as a whole, exists to foster and promote this growth.
3. Christ and my growth in the likeness of Christ must be at the heart of this formation. Any behavior contrary to this principle is unacceptable. Therefore, I deem intolerable such behaviors as:
   a. Drunkenness, vulgarity, and rudeness
   b. Gossip, slander, backbiting, and uncharitable remarks about others
   c. Sexual activity, including inappropriate touching, flirtation, sexual remarks, and innuendos
4. I am guided in my behavior toward others by principles of Christian charity and a spirit of collaboration and mutual regard.
5. I resolve differences between and among others in a mature manner—that is, through person-to-person encounters and open, fair discussions between the parties involved.
6. I avoid malice at all times.
7. I regularly examine my conscience and critique my own behaviors.

Internet Policy

By clarifying an Internet policy, a seminary or formation program can reserve the right to monitor all computer use at any time.

1. The Internet is a tool for intellectual, academic, and personal information and enjoyment.
2. The Internet must not be used to transmit, retrieve, or store any type of communication, message, image, or material that is:
   a. Discriminatory or harassing
   b. Derogatory or inflammatory with respect to race, age, disability, religion, national origin, or physical attributes
   c. Obscene or X-rated
   d. Abusive, profane or offensive language
3. The Internet must not be used for any illegal or immoral reasons.

Code of Ethics for Pastoral Ministry

Some dioceses in the United States have developed codes for pastoral ministry. Many of these tend to be statements of policy, procedures, and liability. Many Protestant denominations have also developed similar codes and they tend to emphasize the behavior of the pastor toward a client. In addition, a number of U.S. companies have developed codes that tend to indicate appropriate and inappropriate employee/employer behaviors.

A code of ethics for pastoral ministry, on the other hand, should emerge out of an ecclesiology based on *Presbyterorum ordinis* (1965) and *Pastores Dabo Vobis* (1992): a priest is called to live a life of human and spiritual wholeness and holiness while serving the Church and the world with new challenges and needs. Consequently, in order for a code of ethics for pastoral ministry to function well in the context of Roman Catholic priesthood, it must serve:

1. As an instrument of self-reflection and be a "constant" in the priest's life.

2. As an index of how a priest should live out his vocation.
3. As a self-assessment, an aide, that identifies "red flags" in a priest's life which, when recognized, must be brought to one's spiritual director, priest support group, counselor, and so on. The aim is to help the priest to integrate the values set forth in the code.

Sample Code of Ethics

Preamble

We recognize the great commandment to love God above all else and to love one's neighbor as oneself as the foundation of our Christian discipleship and of our priesthood. We firmly believe that our relationships with self, others, and God are closely interrelated. Therefore, we must demonstrate the way to love God and neighbor through our own behaviors. We seek to take responsibility for our behaviors by frequently assessing our emotional, spiritual, physical, and psychological needs and how well we attend to these needs. We strive to take care of ourselves in order to be free to attend to the needs of others. We realize that if we do not address our needs, we will not be fully available to serve others. We agree that following these principles are necessary to live according to the gospel.

Self

1. We seek to be physically healthy through proper exercise and nutrition. We guard against self-indulgent behaviors: for example, overeating, abuse of alcohol and prescription drugs.
2. We attend to our emotional health through getting sufficient sleep, taking days off, and vacations.
3. We seek to address our personal need for intimacy through healthy adult relationships outside our pastoral work: for example, with family, friends, and colleagues. We affirm that personal needs must not be met through vulnerable adults or minors.
4. We seek spiritual health through a regular discipline of silence, public and private prayer, reflection and other practices that nurture our relationships with God.

5. We avoid any and all sexual behaviors that would be inconsistent with our commitment to chaste celibacy.

6. We seek guidance regarding moral issues and appropriate boundaries through various sources: for example, spiritual direction, support groups consisting of colleagues, and therapy.

7. We seek to manage and prioritize our time in such a way that we fulfill our responsibility to care for ourselves and to serve others.

8. We acknowledge the need to keep public functions separate from our personal lives as a way of maintaining appropriate boundaries. When this is not possible, we make our personal space available to the public for a particular purpose and for a particular period of time. With regard to the rectory or official living residence, a door may serve as a barrier between personal and public space.

9. We maintain that any relationships with minors outside designated church functions or family visits are always inappropriate.

10. We define and maintain appropriate boundaries in our personal lives so as to live physically, emotionally, and spiritually healthy lives, promote the message of the gospel, and avoid harm to others, either directly or indirectly. We conduct ourselves in a manner consistent with our vocation.

Others

1. We acknowledge the basic dignity of others as being created in the image and likeness of God.

2. We aim to serve others in the image of Jesus Christ through detachment, nondefensiveness, flexibility, acceptance of diversity, and the preservation of human dignity.

3. We seek ways to serve others effectively through the continual development of our theological knowledge and pastoral skills: for example, private study and reading, participating in workshops, professional courses, and sabbaticals.

4. We maintain an environment where we are approachable and available to the community.

5. We strive to be aware of our own vulnerabilities and the vulner-

abilities of others as they pertain to a priest's relationship with a parishioner, counselee, staff, pupil, and so forth. We define and maintain clear boundaries regarding these issues so as not to exploit the trust of those we serve. We guard against having our personal needs met in our pastoral relationships. We seek self-awareness regarding these issues through our various support systems.

6. We seek to avoid dual relationships that may compromise our professional judgment. We monitor our role and boundaries in such a way as to avoid potential exploitation.

7. We seek to be aware of our vulnerabilities regarding sexuality in order to avoid any implicit or explicit sexual misconduct. We do not participate in any sexual behavior for any reason.

8. We guard against the exploitation of others by reporting any sexual misconduct to the appropriate ecclesial and civil authorities.

9. We strive to maintain a safe environment for persons to express themselves by adhering to confidentiality. We keep all confidential material in a locked place and provide an appropriate space for counseling and consultation. We do not participate in gossip nor do we condone this behavior among parish employees.

10. We affirm the absolute confidentiality regarding the seal of confession as outlined in *The Code of Canon Law*. We acknowledge that information obtained through the sacrament of reconciliation may not be implicitly or explicitly disclosed.

Exploitation in Pastoral Ministry

We seek to live by the abovementioned values and principles so as to prevent the exploitation of others in our pastoral relationships. We guard against the following forms and types of exploitation:

1. Providing special attention to particular people (for example, individual parishioners, counselees, staff members, or pupils) that is not offered to others.

2. Attempting to get our personal needs met through these ministerial relationships.

3. Exceeding our own limitations and abilities or inappropriately

taking on other roles outside the boundaries of our priestly ministry: for example, being a parent, therapist, and buddy.

4. Participating in sexual misconduct including, but not limited to, viewing or disseminating sexually explicit images; implicit or explicit sexual speech; implicit or explicit sexual gestures or contact that violates or exploits the boundaries of another person; inviting, manipulating, coercing, or threatening another person in order to obtain sexual favors; physical contact that is aimed at satisfying our own needs; or any other behaviors that may be inconsistent with our commitment to chaste celibacy.

Appendix Two
A Sexual History

Family of Origin

Goal: To obtain an understanding of broad family attitudes about sexuality. In all individuals, the single most important circumstance determinative of affective and sexual development is the family environment. The interviewer should look for signs of discomfort regarding sexuality in the family of origin. Such discomfort is likely passed on to the candidate from the familial environment.

1. Was sexuality discussed openly by your parents, extended family, or older siblings? What was said about sexuality?
2. How comfortable were family members in discussing sex and sexuality?
3. What messages, direct or tacit, were conveyed about sexuality in your family?
4. How did you learn the facts of life (sex/sexuality/reproduction)?
5. Were there any other persons in your family or early life whose attitudes about sexuality affected you? Who were these persons? What were their attitudes? How did their attitudes affect you?

Prepubescent Sexual Development

Goal: To obtain an understanding of the person's earliest sexual feelings and experiences. Early sexual stimulation is a risk factor for later sexual problems. An absence of curiosity about sex and a lack of awareness of sexual interests can be risk factors for later sexual problems, such as unintegrated sexuality.

1. At what age were you first aware of sexual feelings?
2. When did you first have crushes, interests, or curiosity about others?
3. Were you involved in any early childhood sexual play or exploration? Describe each experience, including the ages and genders of other participants, your age at the time, and your feelings about your behavior. Who initiated it? Where did it occur? Did you feel guilty?
4. Did you ever feel pressured by an adult to behave in stereotypically masculine or feminine ways (for example, as a male, being forced to play sports in which you had no interest or talent)? If so, who pressured you? How did you feel? Did you feel that you were a disappointment to that person?

Sexual Abuse History

Goal: To determine if the person has experienced any sexual abuse and/or exploitation. It is important to gain a factual history of any such experiences and an understanding of their impact on the candidate, both physically and emotionally. How sexual abuse was dealt with by the individual and the family can give insights into the family and the candidate's role within it.

1. When you were growing up, did anyone older than you ever touch you or look at you in a way that was blatantly or overtly sexual, or that you experienced as unwanted or intrusive? If so, describe the specific incident, the frequency, the duration, your age and the age of the other person at the time, and your relationship with the other person.
2. How did you feel about that sexual experience? What do you think about it now?
3. Did you ever tell anyone about the experience or discuss it with anyone? If yes, who did you tell? How did the person respond? What happened? If you did not speak to anyone about it, why have you remained silent?
4. As a child or adolescent were you ever involved in any sexual play, exploration, fondling, masturbation, or sexual exposure with

someone younger than yourself? What were the age and gender of the other person(s)? Who initiated the sexual play? Were you ever caught? How did you feel about the experience? How do you think the other person(s) felt about the experience?

Puberty and Adolescence

Goal: To obtain an understanding of the person's sexual development during adolescence, particularly with regard to puberty and masturbatory history. Sexual deviancy often shows its first signs in adolescence. People with excessive sexual involvement during adolescence, as well as people who report no sexual curiosity or sexual challenges during adolescence, may have sexual problems.

1. Were you prepared for the bodily changes you experienced during the onset of puberty? Did anyone talk to you about what would happen to your body or what to expect?
2. How old were you when you entered puberty? What was the experience like? What were your parents' reactions to your puberty?
3. How did you feel about the changes in your body? Did you feel self-conscious around your peers? Did you feel like you were developing or maturing at the same rate as your peers?
4. Were you ever teased or singled out by peers for being different?
5. How old were you when you had your first nocturnal emission? Did you know what it was? What were your feelings about it? Do you remember what your sexual fantasies were at the time of the emission?
6. Did anyone talk with you about masturbation? What were you told about masturbation? How old were you when you first masturbated? How did you feel about it? Did you feel guilty? Did you know that other people did it?
7. What were the fantasies you had when you first masturbated? What fantasies did you usually have during subsequent masturbations?
8. Did you discuss masturbation with peers at any stage? How frequent was masturbation in adolescence, or whenever it first began?

9. During adolescence, did you ever masturbate with others? Were you ever involved in group masturbation? If so, what were the ages and genders of the participants? Who initiated the experience? What was the frequency and duration?

Sexual Orientation

Goal: To obtain an understanding of the person's awareness of his sexual orientation and his acceptance of that orientation.

1. Can you remember any sexual dreams you have had? What genders and approximate ages were the figures in the dreams?
2. What is your sexual orientation? How do you know what your sexual orientation is? What are the concrete signs you use to interpret your sexual orientation? Are you comfortable with your sexual orientation?
3. Have you ever felt curious about or been sexually aroused by, or could you have been sexually aroused by, members of your own sex? Did you ever tell anyone? Did you try to hide it?
4. What was the attitude in your family about homosexuality? How did you feel about that attitude?
5. What was, and currently is, your attitude about homosexuality?
6. If you were going to enter into a genital sexual encounter, what type of person would you prefer for a partner?
7. How old were you when you discovered your sexual orientation? Describe the situation.
8. How did you feel at the time about your sexual orientation? If you had feelings of attraction toward individuals of your own gender, what did you think these feelings said about you?

Dating and Adult Sexual Activity

Goal: To obtain an understanding of the person's experience of dating and adult sexual activity. If a person's sexuality is unintegrated or unbalanced in any way, this will frequently be indicated in his sexual behavior. Extremes such as repression of all sexual feelings or compulsive sexual activity should cause concern.

1. Have you ever dated? Who were your partners? Was there any sexual contact? How old were you?
2. Have you ever been in love? How old were you and the other person? What was the gender of the other person? Describe the relationship between you and this person. What happened to the relationship?
3. Has marriage ever been an option for you? Would you like it to be?
4. Have you ever been married? What was your marriage like for you? What is your present relationship with your former wife (if she is alive)? What leads you to think that you do not want to marry again in the future? Have you ever fathered any children? What has your responsibility for them been like?
5. When was your last sexual contact?
6. How frequently do you masturbate? What are your fantasies?
7. Have you ever had a sexual encounter with someone you did not know before that time? How often have such encounters occurred? Where did you meet the person(s) involved? Describe the events leading up to the encounters, their frequency and location, and the sexual behavior that occurred.
8. Have you ever been tested or treated for a sexually transmitted disease? Have you ever been tested for HIV or AIDS? If so, why did you feel the need for testing?

Paraphilia and Other Problematic Sexual Behavior

Goal: To determine if the person has engaged in sexually deviant or problematic behavior. The presence of previous deviant sexual behavior or a deviant sexual arousal pattern is cause for considerable concern and should be investigated as thoroughly as possible.

1. Did you ever engage in any sexual behavior that others might consider unusual? If so, please describe.

2. Have you ever paid someone for sex? If so, explain.

3. Have you ever read "adult" magazines, magazines with pictures of children, or magazines that others might consider to be pornographic? What were the magazines? How often do you use them? What ages and genders are the people shown? When was the last time you looked at one?

4. Have you ever visited an adult bookstore? If yes, when was the last time you visited one? How often did or do you go? What exactly did you (or do you) do inside?

5. Did you ever engage in any other sexual behavior, such as exposing yourself to other people? If yes, please describe.

6. Have you ever taken minors on vacations, on overnight trips, out to dinner, or other private functions? If yes, please describe. Were any other adults present?

7. As an adult, have you ever slept in the same bed or shared overnight accommodations with any minors?

8. Have you ever found yourself, when masturbating, thinking about people you have known who are under the age of eighteen? Have you ever had other sexual fantasies about people under the age of eighteen? Have you ever found yourself attracted to or aroused by young people? Please describe the situation and age of the young person.

9. Has anyone ever suggested or alleged that you had a sexual encounter with someone under the age of eighteen?

10. Have you ever been in a situation where you could have or did become sexually aroused or acted inappropriately with someone under the age of eighteen? If so, what was your relationship with the minor? How old were you at that time? What happened?

12. Have you ever had a sexual encounter with someone with whom you had a supervisory relationship (for example, teacher/student, pastoral minister/parishioner, counselor/counselee, employer/employee)?

13. Do you find some things or activities sexually arousing that other people might consider different or unusual?

Current Management of Sexual Behavior and Feelings

Goal: To understand how the person experiences, manages, and integrates his sexual feelings, especially in light of chaste celibacy lifestyle. Areas of concern include an absence of sexual awareness, a spiritualization of sexuality, excessive scruples and/or moralizing about sexuality, compulsive sexual behavior, and denial of sexual feelings.

1. How do you currently experience your sexual desires or innate sexuality?
2. When are you aware of yourself as a sexual person?
3. How do you understand and respond to your sexual desires?
4. What challenges regarding your sexuality do you currently face? How are you attempting to deal with these challenges?
5. Are you able to fulfill a desire for nurturance and love in your life?
6. Who is your closest friend? How often do you see each other? What do you do and talk about together?
7. Do you have any physical contact with other people? Please describe.
8. How do you understand the commitment to celibacy?
9. How should celibates deal with their sexuality?
10. Do you think you will be able to live a life of celibate chastity and be at peace with such a lifestyle?
11. What difficulties and struggles do you think you will experience in trying to live celibate chastity?
12. What will be the joys and rewards of a celibate life?
13. What do you think would happen if you fell in love?

Sexual Abuse of Minors: Signs and Cautions[1]

Warning Signs of Preferential Offenders

1. Finds reasons to spend times with minors.
2. Prefers time with minors to time with peers.
3. Gives gifts to minors, especially without permission.
4. Goes overboard with physical contact with minors.
5. Wants to wrestle or tickle minors.
6. Shows favoritism toward minors.
7. Treats minors like equals.
8. Keeps secrets with minors.
9. Ignores policies about interacting with minors.
10. Uses inappropriate language with minors.
11. Tells off-color jokes to minors.

Warning Signs of Situational Offenders

1. Excessive use of alcohol.
2. Use of drugs.
3. Experiencing anxiety, depression, stress.
4. Having trouble with loneliness.
5. Is facing rejection or disappointment.
6. Is coping with personal loss.
7. Feels unappreciated and unrewarded for work.
8. Becomes increasingly dependent on a relationship with a minor, especially one who is convenient, for example, works in the house.

Behaviors That Have Led to False Accusations

1. Meeting others in isolated places.
2. Showing favoritism.
3. Engaging in physical contact that was misunderstood.
4. Wearing provocative and revealing clothes.
5. Giving money to a special minor.
6. Meeting in homes or bedrooms with a minor with no one else present.
7. Sleeping in bed with minors.
8. Graphically discussing sexual activities with minors.
9. Giving special or secret gifts.
10. Keeping secrets about relationships.
11. Failing to adhere to accepted standards of affection.
12. Showing affection when no one else is present.
13. Staring while others are dressing.
14. Commenting on a minor's body.
15. Taking pictures while minors are dressing or showering.
16. Shaming or belittling an individual.

Inappropriate Displays of Affection

1. Any form of unwanted affection.
2. Frontal hugs or bear hugs.
3. Touching bottoms, chests, or genital areas.
4. Laying down or sleeping with minors.
5. Massages.
6. Patting children on the thigh, knee, or leg.
7. Tickling or wrestling.
8. Touching or hugging from behind.
9. Games involving inappropriate touching.
10. Kisses on the mouth.
11. Showing affection in isolated places, for example, bedrooms, closets, restricted areas.
12. Compliments that relate to physique or body development.

Notes

Abbreviations

BPOFP *The Basic Plan for the Ongoing Formation of Priests*
CCC *Catechism of the Catholic Church*
CCL *Corpus Christianorum, Series Latina*
CDF Congregation for the Doctrine of the Faith
Charter *Charter for the Protection of Children and Young People*
CLSA *The Code of Canon Law*
Essential Norms
  *Essential Norms for Diocesan/Eparchial Policies Dealing
  with Allegations of Sexual Abuse of Minors by Priests, Deacons, or
  Other Church Personnel*
PDV *Pastores Dabo Vobis*
PPF *Program of Priestly Formation*
USCCB United States Conference of Catholic Bishops

Foreword

1. See, for example, Donald B. Cozzens, *The Changing Face of the Priesthood: A Reflection on the Priest's Crisis of Soul* (Collegeville, Minn.: Liturgical Press, 2000); Marie M. Fortune and Merle Longwood, eds., *Sexual Abuse in the Catholic Church* (Binghamton, N.Y.: Haworth Pastoral Press, 2003); Andrew Greeley, *Priests: A Calling in Crisis* (Chicago: University of Chicago Press, 2004); Philip Jenkins, *Pedophiles and Priests: Anatomy of a Contemporary Crisis* (New York: Oxford University Press, 2001); Thomas G. Plante, *Sin against the Innocents: Sexual Abuse by Priests and the Role of the Catholic Church* (Westport, Conn.: Greenwood, 2004); Thomas G. Plante, ed., *Bless me Father for I Have Sinned: Perspectives on Sexual Abuse Committed by Roman Catholic Priests* (Westport, Conn.: Greenwood, 1999).
2. Andrew Greeley, *Priests: A Calling in Crisis.*

3. See Thomas G. Plante, A. Aldridge, and C. Louie, "Are Successful Applicants to the Priesthood Psychologically Healthy?" *Pastoral Psychology*, in press.

Chapter One

1. Saint Bede the Venerable, *Homily* 21: CCL 122, 149–151. See also the Office of Readings for the Feast of Saint Matthew.

2. *The Basic Plan for the Ongoing Formation of Priests* [hereafter *BPOFP*] (Washington, D.C.: United States Catholic Conference of Bishops [hereafter USCCB], 2001), 1; Pope John Paul II, *Pastores Dabo Vobis* [hereafter *PDV*] in *Origins* 21 (1992), 717–759.

3. Congregation for the Clergy, Directory for the Life and Minstry of Priests (Vatican City: Libreria Editrice Vaticana, 1994).

4. *Program of Priestly Formation,* 5th edition [hereafter *PPF*] (Washington, D.C.: USCCB, forthcoming). *Program of Priestly Formation,* fifth edition, was approved by the U.S. bishops in June 2005. References to the fifth edition do not include pagination references because, as of the date of publication, it has not yet received the *regognitio* of the Holy See.

5. See Pope John Paul II, *PDV,* nos. 43–59.

6. Ibid., no. 44.

7. Ibid., no. 44.

8. *Directory for the Life and Ministry of Priests* (Vatican City: Libreria Editrice Vaticana, 1994), no. 55.

9. Pope John Paul II, *Pastores Gregis* (Vatican City: Libreria Editrice Vaticana, 2003).

10. Karl Rahner, *Servants of the Lord* (New York: Herder and Herder, 1968), 112–113.

11. Thomas Merton, *The Seven Storey Mountain* (New York: Harcourt, Brace & Co., 1968), 410.

12. Pope John Paul II, *Rise, Let Us Be on Our Way* (New York: Warner Books, 2004), 3–56.

13. Ibid., 106.

14. Ibid., 63.

15. Ibid., 135. See also Pope John Paul II, *Radiation of Fatherhood* (Washington, D.C.: USCCB, 2003).

16. Pope John Paul II, *Rise, Let Us Be on Our Way,* 127.

Chapter Two

1. Congregation for the Clergy, *Directory for the Life and Ministry of Priests* (Vatican City: Libreria Editrice Vaticana, 1994), no. 38.
2. Pope John Paul II, *PDV*, no. 33.
3. George Aschenbrenner, SJ, "Portrait of the Authentic Celibate in Our American Culture," *Seminary Journal* 10 (2004): 7–18, citation at 7.
4. See, for example, Donald B. Cozzens, *The Changing Face of the Priesthood.*
5. Tony Hendra, *Father Joe: The Man Who Saved My Soul* (New York: Random House, 2004), 4.
6. Hendra, *Father Joe*, 76, 57.
7. Pope John Paul II, *PDV*, no. 28.
8. Ibid., no. 19.
9. See "Decree on the Ministry and Life of Priests" (1965) in *Vatican Council II*, edited by Austin Flannery, OP (New York: Costello Publishing Co., 1975), 863–902.
10. These observations are based on the thoughts of James W. Fowler, "You Bet Your Life: Finding Meaning, and Perhaps, Vocation," *The Santa Clara Lectures* 10 (2003).
11. Frederick Buechner, *Wishful Thinking* (New York: Harper and Row, 1984), cited in Fowler, 2.
12. Lewis Carroll, *The Annotated Alice*, introduction and notes by Martin Gardner (New York: W.W. Norton & Company, 1960), 65.
13. Fowler, "You Bet Your Life," 14.
14. Ibid., 18.
15. See *PPF*, 5th edition.
16. Pope John Paul II, Homily, Feast of the Annunciation, May 2004.
17. Pope John Paul II, *Rise, Let Us Be on Our Way*, 215.
18. Ibid., 213.
19. Quoted in Howard P. Bleichner, SS, *View from the Altar: Reflections on the Rapidly Changing Catholic Priesthood* (New York: Crossroad, 2004), 209.
20. See Aschenbrenner, "Portrait of the Authentic Celibate in Our American Culture," 9.
21. See Eugene Hemrick, "The Heart of a Wholesome Priesthood," *Seminary Journal* 10 (2004): 39–41.
22. See Len Sperry, *Sex, Priestly Ministry, and the Church* (Collegeville, Minn.: Liturgical Press, 2003), 66–67.
23. For a helpful overview of the theology of the priesthood from the Council of Trent (1545–1563) to the present time, see Bleichner, *View from the Altar*, 19–59, 138–164.

24. Ibid., 31.

25. See, for example, *Lumen Gentium*, no. 10.

26. Ibid., no. 21.

27. Bleichner, *View from the Altar*, 145.

28. Ibid., 154.

29. Ibid., 156–164.

30. Conversion keeps a seminarian or priest from "reverting to type" after ordination. See Dennis Sheehan, "Formation for a Holy, Healthy, Effective Priesthood," *Origins* 34 (2004): 71–76.

31. Ibid., 73.

32. Bernard Lonergan, *Method in Theology* (New York: Herder and Herder, 1982), 267–69.

33. See *BPOFP*, part two. This plan divides the threefold process into (1) the first years of priesthood; (2) changes of assignment; (3) first pastorates, priests at midlife, and senior clergy.

Chapter Three

1. Interestingly, Protestant seminarians and clergy were also identified as professionals. However, like their Catholic peers, in recent years they have moved from "professional" to "deprofessionalized." See Sherryl Kleinman, *Equals Before God: Seminarians as Humanistic Professionals* (Chicago: The University of Chicago Press, 1984).

2. See John Tracy Ellis, "The Formation of the American Priest: A Historical Perspective," in *The Catholic Priest in the United States* (Collegeville, Minn.: St. John's University Press, 1971).

3. Dean Hoge and Jacqueline Wenger, *Evolving Visions of the Priesthood* (Collegeville, Minn.: Liturgical Press, 2003). See also, Gerald D. Coleman, "Recapturing Priestly Joy," in *Evolving Visions of the Priesthood*, 183–190.

4. Summary of "Entrance Interviews," 1994–2004, Archives of St. Patrick's Seminary and University, Menlo Park, California.

5. Katarina Schuth, *Seminaries, Theologates, and the Future of Church Ministry* (Collegeville, Minn.: The Liturgical Press, 1999) and her unpublished document "Vocation, Seminarians, Initial Formation, and Continuing Education/Formation of Priests: Some Information and Questions," 2003.

6. John C, Kemper, SS, "The Priestly Formation of Generation X," *Human Development* 21 (2000): 14–19.

7. See the video "Time for Tea: A Drink of Asian Culture," produced by the National Religious Conference, 2000.

8. See Gary Riebe-Estrella, "American Cultural Shifts: Formation for Which Candidates? For Which Church?" *Seminary Journal* 2 (1996): 27–33.

9. Ibid., 30.

10. Bleichner, *View from the Altar*, 62–63, 67. See also *PDV*, Part 2.

11. Pope John Paul II, *PDV*, no. 62.

12. Ibid., no. 69.

13. Ibid., nos. 71–72.

14. Len Sperry, *Sex, Priestly Ministry, and the Church* (Collegeville, Minn.: Liturgical Press, 2003), 119–137.

15. Stephen A. Buglione, "Screening Revisited: Issues in the Psychological Assessment of Seminary Applicants," *Seminary Journal* 9 (2003): 59.

16. Buglione stresses the "importance of ruling out personality pathology in seminary selection…since such individuals (e.g., anti-social, narcissistic, and borderline individuals)—often having histories of abuse, neglect or other emotionally traumatic experiences, together with serious impairments in empathy, impulse control, and judgment—tend to be at high risk for violating interpersonal boundaries, including predatory behavior." See Buglione, "Screening Revisited," 61.

17. Gerald D. Coleman, SS, and Roger L. Freed, MD, "Assessing Seminary Candidates," *Human Development* 21 (1999): 14–20. See also PDV, no. 62.

18. Merlvin C. Blanchette, SS, "On Screening Seminarians Through Behavioral Assessment and Psychological Testing," *Seminary Journal* 3 (1997): 9–34.

19. See Thomas G. Plante, "Are Successful Applicants to the Priesthood Psychologically Healthy," *Pastoral Psychology* 54 (September 2005): 81–90. Plante analyzes the MMPI-2 and 16PF administered to sixty-eight applicants to major Roman Catholic religious orders between 1990 and 2004. Negative tendencies are indicated in terms of some defensiveness, repression, anger, and hostility. General results indicate that these applicants to the priesthood were generally well-adjusted, socially responsible, interpersonally sensitive, and sociable.

20. See Blanchette for a more detailed analysis, ibid., 17–34.

21. See Coleman and Freed, "Assessing Seminary Candidates," esp. 14–15.

22. Herman J. Pottmeyer, "Reception of Doctrine," in *Encyclopedia of Catholicism*, ed., Richard McBrien (San Francisco: HarperCollins, 1995), 1081–1082.

Chapter Four

1. See Saint Ignatius of Antioch, "Letter to the Romans," 4, 1–2; 6:1–8 in *Ancient Christian Writers: the Epistles of Saint Clement of Rome and Saint Ignatius of Antioch,* edited by James A. Kleist (Mahwah, N.J.: Paulist Press, 1978).

2. William J. Hoye, "A Transparent Philosopher," *America* 191 (2004): 16–22.

3. See *BPOFP* (2001), 24–26.

4. In *View from the Altar*, 90–91. Howard Bleichner wisely offers the maxim, "Take care of your physical health" by a set of habits such as regular exercise, proper diet, moderation in drinking. These habits will assist one in keeping vigilance over one's body. Bleichner comments, "If a seminarian neglects his physical health now, the problem only grows worse later."

5. See Jude P. Dougherty, "The Ordinary and Extraordinary in Priestly Formation," *Seminarium* 3 (2000): 607–615.

6. Ibid., 612. Also see Paul Ritt, "Three Challenges for Seminary and Ongoing Education," *Origins* 34 (2004): 76–79.

7. *BPOFP*, 11–26.

8. Ibid., 39–89.

9. See Cornelius Hubbuck, "Productive Attitudes to Growing Older," *Covenant* 18 (2004): 3–4.

10. See Gerald A. Arbuckle, SM, "Seminary Formation as a Pilgrimage," *Human Development* 7 (1986): 27–33.

11. See Clifford Geertz, *The Interpretation of Cultures: selected essays* (New York: Basic Books, 1973).

12. See "George Aschenbrenner, SJ, "Presumption for Perseverance and Permanence: A Rudder for Direction and Balance in Priestly Formation," *Seminary Journal* 4.1 (1998): 17–25.

13. See Hermann J. Pottmeyer, "Reception and Submission," *Jurist* 51 (1991): 262–292.

14. The preface of the *PPF* outlines the many documents of the Holy See and the U.S. Bishops that have dealt with the meaning of the priestly office. These documents form an important backdrop for the new edition of the *PPF*.

15. C.K. Chesterton, *Orthodoxy* (New York: Finage Books, Doubleday, 1990), 81–101, especially 83. As quoted in Bleichner, *View from the Altar*, 115.

16. Harold S. Kushner, *How Good Do We Have To Be?* (Boston: Little, Brown & Co., 1996), 77–78.

17. Ronald Rolheiser, "Beauty Has the Power to Transform Us," in *Western Catholic Reporter* (July 19, 1999).

18. Daniel O'Leary, "Beauty and the Priest," *The Tablet* (September 18, 2004): 10.

19. See Anne Hine, "Ministry – Formation – Training," *The Way Supplement*, 56 (1986): 85–96.

20. See Louis J. Cameli, S.T.D., "Origins and Promise: Perspectives on Human Formation," *Seminary Journal* 1.2 (1995): 9–18.

21. Ibid., nos. 43–44.

22. Ibid., 14. Cameli here cites the works of William Meissner and Paul Ricoeur.

23. See Jean Laplace, *Preparing for Spiritual Direction*, trans. John C. Guinness (Chicago: Franciscan Herald Press, 1975), 33–34.

24. Cameli, "Origins and Promise," 16.

25. George Aschenbrenner, SJ, "Gold Purified in Fire: Diocesan Seminary Formation," *Seminary Journal* 3.3 (1997): 51.

26. Ibid.

27. Ibid., 55–56.

28. See Henri Nouwen, *The Way of the Heart* (New York: Seabury Press, 1981), 19–44.

29. See Richard M. Liddy, "Formation: Developing Habits of the Mind and Heart," *Seminary Journal* 1.3 (1995): 20–30.

30. Ibid., 29.

31. See Wayne Muller, *Sabbath: Restoring the Sacred Rhythm of Rest* (New York: Bantam, 1999).

32. See Frank P. Lane, "The Seminarian and the World: What Is Formation?" *Josephinum Journal of Theology* 8 (2001): 166–168. Lane here references Piet F. Fransen, SJ, "Man and Freedom" in *Man Before God: Toward a Theology of Man*, ed., Denis Burkhard, et al (New York: Kenedy, 1966), 81.

33. See John F. Canary, "The Seminary as a Context for Modeling the Integrated Life," *Seminary Journal* 4.3 (1998): 45–59.

34. James J. Gill, SJ, "Too Many Casualties," *Human Development* 21 (2000): 3–4.

35. See Gerald T. Broccolo and Ernest E. Larkin, eds., *Spiritual Renewal of the American Priesthood* (Washington, D.C.: USCCB, 1973), 114. Also see Daniel Danielson, "Priestly Spirituality in Our Day," *Seminary Journal* 10 (2004): 24–27.

36. Edward J. Farrell, *The Father Is Very Fond of Me* (Denville, N.J.: Dimension Books, 1975), 5.

Chapter Five

1. James Nelson, *The Intimate Connection: Male Sexuality and Masculine Spirituality and Embodiment* (Philadelphia: Westminster Press, 1988), 26.

2. Sacred Congregation for Catholic Education, "Educational Guidance in Human Love: Outlines for Sex Education" (Vatican City: Libreria Editrice Vaticana, 1983), no. 4.

3. See William Kraft, *Sexual Dimensions of the Celibate Life* (Kansas City, Mo.: Andrews and McMeel, 1979).

4. James R. Zullo, "Educating Seminarians for Healthy Sociality," *Seminary Journal* 1.2 (1995): 39.

5. Mark Patrick Hederman, *Manikon Eros: Mad Crazy Love* (Dublin: Veritas Publications, 2000), 66.

6. Saint Thomas Aquinas, *Commentary of the Sentences* III, 25, 1.1, 4.

7. C.S. Lewis, *The Four Loves* (New York: Harcourt, Brace & World, 1960), 111.

8. Timothy Radcliff, "Afectividad y Eucaristia," unpublished paper, 3.

9. Len Sperry, *Sex, Priestly Ministry, and the Church* (Collegeville, Minn., Liturgical Press), 2003.

10. Ibid., 5–6.

11. Ibid., 23–24.

12. Ibid., 52.

13. See Thomas Plante and Kieran Sullivan, *Getting Together and Staying Together: The Stanford University Course on Intimate Relationships* (Stanford: 1stBooks Library-rev, 2001), 15.

14. See Tomas Andres, *Understanding the Filipino* (Quezon City, Philippines: New Day Publishers, 1987); Joseph Carrier, *De Los Otros* (New York: Columbia Press, 1995); David Abalos, *The Latino Male* (Boulder: Lynne Reinner Press, 2002); and Marit Melhuus and Kristi Anne Stolen, *Machos, Mistresses, and Madonnas* (New York: Verso, 1996).

15. See David Ranson, "Sexual Abuse," *The Furrow* 4 (2000): 223–229.

16. Peter Rutter, *Sex in the Forbidden Zone* (New York: McMillan Co., 1986).

17. See John Bradshaw, *Healing the Shame That Binds You* (Deerfield Beach, Florida: Health Communications, Inc., 1988); J.W. Schneider, "Shame" in *Dictionary of Pastoral Counseling*, ed., Rodney J. Hunter (Nashville: Abington Press, 1990); and Lewis B. Smedes, *Shame and Grace* (San Francisco: Harper, 1993).

18. See Gerald D. Coleman, "Taking a Sexual History," *Human Development* 17 (1996): 10–15. This history has been adopted by some seminarians and religious communities in the United States.

19. Sperry, *Sex, Priestly Ministry, and the Church*, 58, table 3–4.

20. *BPOFP*, 39–89.

21. W.T. Reich, ed., "Homosexuality," in *Encyclopedia of Bioethics*, vol. 2 (New York: The Free Press, 1992), 671.

22. *Catechism of the Catholic Church* [hereafter *CCC*] (Vatican City: Libreria Editrice Vaticana, 1997), no. 2357.

23. Congregation for the Doctrine of the Faith [hereafter CDF] *Letter to the Bishops of the Catholic Church on the Pastoral Care of Homosexual Persons* (Vatican City: Libreria Editrice Vaticana, 1996), 3.

24. Ibid., 16.

25. See Len Sperry, "The Homosexual Debate," *Human Development* 23 (2002): 8–12.

26. Ibid., 9.

27. John R. Allen Jr., "Homosexuality as a Risk Factor," *National Catholic Reporter*, April 18, 2003. See James F. Keenan, SJ, "Notes on Moral Theology," Theological Studies 66 (2005), 125.

28. Guidelines and references set forth in the fifth edition of the *PPF* must be followed regarding admission of homosexual candidates to seminaries and houses of formation. See also the Congregation for Catholic Education, "Instruction Concerning the Criteria for the Discernment of Vocations With Regard to Persons With Homosexual Tendencies in View of Their Admission to the Seminary and to Sacred Orders," *Origins* 35, no. 26 (December 8, 2005): 429–32.

29. Congregation for Catholic Education, "Instruction Concerning Criteria for the Discernment of Vocations with Regard to Persons with Homosexual Tendencies in View of Their Admission to the seminary and to Holy Orders," (Vatican City: Libreria Editrice Vaticana, 2005), no. 2.

30. See *CCC*, nos.1808–1809.

31. Saint Augustine, *De moribus eccl.* 1, 25, 46, in *Patrologia Latina* 32, 1330–1331.

32. See Paul J. Wadell, *Friendship and the Moral Life* (Notre Dame: University of Notre Dame Press, 1989), 1–8, and "The Role of Friendship in the Moral and Spiritual Development of Seminarians," *Seminary Journal* 1 (1995): 19–29.

33. See Jules Toner, *Love and Friendship* (Milwaukee: Marquette University Press, 2003).

34. Wilkie Au, "Particular Friendships Revisited," *Human Development* 7 (1986): 34–38.

35. Charles M. Shelton, "Friendship in Jesuit Life," *Studies in the Spirituality of Jesuits* 27/5 (1995): 1–42.

36. Ibid., 29.

37. Ronald Rolheiser, *The Restless Heart* (New York; Doubleday, 2004), 3.

38. John of the Cross, *The Ascent of Mount Carmel* 1: 6–10, translated by Kieran Kavanaugh, in *The Collected Works of St. John of the Cross* (Washington, D.C.: Institute of Carmelite Studies, 1973).

39. See Thomas Moore, *Dark Nights of the Soul* (New York: Gotham Books, 2004).

40. John of the Cross, "The Dark Night," in *The Collected Works of St. John of the Cross,* stanza 5, 1–2. .

41. Henri Nouwen, *Reaching Out* (New York: Image, 1986).

42. See Karen Lebacqz, *Professional Ethics* (Nashville: Abingdon Press, 1992); and Paul B. Macke, "Boundaries in Ministerial Relationships," *Human Development* 14 (1993), 23–25.

Chapter Six

1. Both reports were published on the same day, February 27, 2004. The following highlights Howard P. Bleichner interpretation of the findings in *View From the Altar*, 43–44.

2. Pope John Paul II, "Address to the Cardinals of the United States," April 23, 2004.

3. See Thomas Plante, *Bless Me Father for I Have Sinned: Perspectives on Sexual Abuse Committed by Roman Catholic Priests* (Westport, Conn.: Praeger, 1999), and *Sin Against the Innocents* (Westport, Conn.: Praeger, 2004).

4. See *Charter for the Protection of Children and Young People* [hereafter *Charter*], Washington, D.C.: USCCB, 2002). In June 2005, the U.S. bishops revised the *Charter*. This selection reflects those revisions.

5. Essential Norms for Diocesan/Eparchial Policies Dealing with Allegations of Sexual Abuse of Minors by Priests, Deacons, or Other Church Personnel [hereafter *Essential Norms*], preamble. (Note: text has not yet been confirmed by the Holy See as of publication.)

6. Ibid., note 2.

7. These materials are largely based on James H. Provost, "Offenses Against the Sixth Commandment: Toward a Canonical Analysis of Canon 1395," *The Jurist* 55 (1995): 632–663.

8. See especially *Code of Canon Law* [hereafter *CLSA*), canon 1395.

9. Provost, "Offenses Against the Sixth Commandment," 632–663.

10. *Essential Norms*, no. 4.

11. See *Charter*, preamble, third paragraph.

12. *CLSA*, canon 1321:1. See also John P. Beal, James A. Coriden, Thomas J. Green, eds., *New Commentary on the Code of Canon Law* (Mahwah, N.J.: Paulist Press, 2000).

13. Ibid, no. 1341.

14. Pope John Paul II, "Address to the Cardinals of the United States," April 23, 2004.

15. *Essential Norms*, no. 8.

16. See *Charter*, 8C.

17. *Essential Norms*, no. 8.

18. Vatican II, *Decree on the Liturgy*, no. 7.

19. See Francis Dorf, "Are We Killing Our Priests?" *America* 181 (2000): 7–9.

20. Plante, *Bless Me Father for I Have Sinned*, 46.

21. Statement from the Congregation for the Doctrine of Faith, 1972.

22. *CLSA*, canon 1395:2.

23. Beal, et. al., *New Commentary on the Code of Canon Law*, 1553–1554.

24. John Stuart Mill, *On Liberty* (New Haven, Conn.: Yale University Press, 2003), 121ff.

25. Stephen J. Rossetti, "Priest Suicide and the Crisis of Faith," *America* 171 (1994): 10.

26. See Ray Dlugos, "Repent…and Believe the Good News," *Covenant* 18 (2004): 5.

27. See Paul Duckro and Marc Falkenhain in "Narcissism Sets the Stage for Clergy Sexual Abuse," *Human Development* 3 (2000): 24–28.

28. This description is found in *Diagnostic and Statistical Manual of Mental Disorders* DSM-IV-TR, Fourth Edition (Washington, D.C.: American Psychiatric Association, 2000).

29. See Chris Ashabo, "Addiction Treatment: Beyond Alcohol and Drugs," *Covenant* 18 (2004): 1 and 6.

30. See Kevin P. McClone, "Psychospirituality of Addiction," *Seminary Journal* 9 (2003): 26–33.

31. Ibid., 27.

32. Alcoholics Anonymous, *The Big Book*, Fourth Edition (New York: World Service, Inc., 1952).

33. Ernest and Katherine Kurtz, *A Spirituality of Imperfection* (New York: Bantam Books, 1992).

34. Lewis Presnall, *The Search for Serenity* (Salt Lake City, Utah: UAF Publishing, Utah Alcohol Foundation, 1959). Cited by McClone, "Psychospirituality of Addiction," 31.

35. Patrick J. Carnes, *Out of the Shadows: Understanding Sexual Addiction* (Minneapolis: Hazelden, 2001), 28.

36. See Richard Chiola, "A Case for Teaching Sexual Addiction Assessment to Seminarians: Preparation as Confessors and Spiritual Directors," *Seminary Journal* 9 (2003): 47–52.

37. Karl Rahner identifies the addict's despair and distress as a constitutive sign of sin and guilt. See Rahner, "Guilt and Its Remission: The Borderline Between Theology and Psychotherapy," *Theological Investigations* 2: 9 (Baltimore: Helicon Press, 1963), 265–281.

38. We will closely follow here the insights of David Delmonico and Elizabeth Griffin in "In the Shadows of the Net: Understanding Cybersex in the Seminary," *Seminary Journal* 9 (2003): 39–45. This article likewise refers to many professional studies on this question.

39. Ibid., 40. It should be noted that not everyone who engages in Online Sexual Activity (OSA) is involved at a pathological or problematic level: for example, it has been reported that 70 to 75 percent of adolescents reported using the

Internet to get sexual information for either self-knowledge or assigned research projects.

40. Ibid., 41.
41. Delmonico, Griffin, and Moriarty, "In the Shadows of the Net," 42.
42. Pontifical Council for Social Communications, The *Church and the Internet*
    (Vatican City: Libreria Editrice Vaticana, 2002), no. 7. See also Richard Davis,
    "A Cognitive-Behavioral Model of Pathological Internet Use," *Computers in
    Human Behavior* 17 (2001): 187–195.
43. See James A. Rafferty, "Internet Addiction and Seminary Formation," *Semi-
    nary Journal* 8 (2002): 24–33.
44. See Stephen Olert and Ruthann Williams, "In a Plain Paper Wrapper: Help
    for the Sex Addict," *Seminary Journal* 9 (2003), 53–58.
45. See Patrick J. Carnes, *Out of the Shadows* and *Facing the Shadow: Starting
    Sexual and Relational Recovery* (Scottsdale: Gentle Path Press, 2001). See also
    Delmonico *et al.*, "In the Shadows of the Net," 39–45.
46. Carnes, *Out of the Shadows*. Cited in Olert and Williams, op. cit., 55.
47. Sexaholics Anonymous follows a twelve-step program and can be of great
    value in helping sexaholics to get and stay "sober" (http://www.sa.org).
48. Kimberly S. Young, "Internet Addiction: The Emergence of a New Clinical
    Disorder," *CyberPsychology and Behavior* 1 (2002): 237–244, and *Caught in
    the Net: How to Recognize the Signs of Internet Addiction and a Winning Strat-
    egy for Recovery* (New York: Wiley, 1998, 2001).
49. See Mark A. Latcovich and Sis Wenger, "A Case Study Approach to Teaching
    Chemical Dependency in Seminary Formation: An Application of the Core
    Competencies," *Seminary Journal* 9 (2003): 20–25.
50. *PDV*, no. 69.
51. Ibid., nos. 78–79. See also *BPOFP*, 11–12.

Chapter Seven

1. *PPF*, 3rd edition, no. 64.
2. *PDV*, no. 50.
3. *CLSA* 277:1.
4. See Ronald D. Witherup, "A Biblical Spirituality of Celibacy," *Seminary Journal* 9 (2003): 43–49.
5. Ladislas M. Orsy, "Reception of Doctrine," *Encyclopedia of Catholicism*, ed.,
   Richard McBrien (San Francisco: HarperCollins, 1995), 1081.
6. Congregation for Catholic Education, *A Guide to Formation in Priestly Celibacy* (Washington, D.C.: USCCB, 1974), nos. 47–49.
7. Ibid., no. 51.

8. *PDV*, no. 50.

9. See Howard P. Bleichner, *View from the Altar*, 108–110.

10. Ibid., 108.

11. Ibid., 109.

12. See David L. Fleming, "Discerning Our Celibate Way in Our Culture," *Seminary Journal* 7 (2001): 10–15.

13. *BPOFP*, 31–33.

14. See Thomas W. Krenik, *Formation for Chaste Celibacy: Seven Essential Guiding Elements*, (Washington, D.C.: National Education Association, 1999).

15. See George Aschenbrenner, "Portrait of the Authentic Celibate in Our American Culture," *Seminary Journal* 10 (2004): 7–18.

16. *BPOFP*, 32.

17. USCCB, *Human Sexuality: A Catholic Perspective for Education and Lifelong Learning* (Washington, D.C.: USCCB, 1991), 19.

18. *CCC*, no. 2337.

19. Ibid., nos. 2338–2347. The *Catechism* lists these offenses against chastity: lust, masturbation, fornication, pornography, prostitution, rape, and homosexual activity. See nos. 2351–2359.

20. For helpful materials, see Pope Paul VI, *Encyclical Letter on Priestly Celibacy* (*Sacerdptalis Caelibatus*) (Washington, D.C.: USCCB, 1967); U.S. Conference of Major Superiors of Men, *Men Vowed and Sexual: Conversations about Celibate Chastity* (video presentation), 1993, and Sean D. Sammon, *An Undivided Heart: Making Sense of Celibate Chastity* (New York: Alba House, 1993).

21. See Gerald D. Coleman, "Zero Tolerance," *Commonweal* 129 (2002), 9.

22. Timothy Radcliff, "Afectividad y Eucaristia," unpublished paper, 4–10.

23. Thomas Aquinas, *Summa Theologica* II-II: 151.1.

24. See Josef Pieper, *The Four Cardinal Virtues* (Notre Dame: Notre Dame University Press, 1966), 156.

25. See above, chapter 5, "Introduction," 61.

26. Pieper, *The Four Cardinal Virtues*, 7.

27. Rainer Maria Rilke and Kathleen Schallock, *Inner Solitude* (Madison, Wis.: Prenstemon Press, 1975), 82.

28. Jean Vanier, *Finding Peace* (Toronto: House of Anasi Press, 2003).

29. See Frederick Leising, "Reflections on Celibacy," *Seminary Journal* 1 (1995): 31–33.

30. Linda Krehmeier, Guadalupe Ramirez, William Jarema, "Celibacy: Rite of Initiation for Beginners," *Seminary Journal* 2 (1996): 58–62.

31. Dorothy Day, *The Long Loneliness* (San Francisco: Harper and Row, 1952), 26.

32. Joyce Rupp, *Praying Our Goodbyes* (Notre Dame, Ind.: Ave Maria Press, 1988).

33. John Paul II, "Church Committed to Priestly Celibacy," *L'Osservatore Romano* (July 21, 1993).

Conclusion

1. William J. Levada, "Vocations Begin With a Love of Jesus," *Catholic San Francisco*, November 5, 2004, 10–11.

2. Ronald Rolheiser, *Against an Infinite Horizon* (New York: Crossroad, 1995, 2001), 49–67.

3. See Roger A. Statnick, "Elements of Spiritual Leadership," *Human Development* 25 (2004): 14–24.

4. Saint Augustine, Sermon 46, 2: CCL 41, 530.

5. Reinhold Niebuhr, see "The Origin of Our Serenity Prayer," http://silkworth .net/aa/Serenity-Prayer-Origin.htm.

6. In the following analysis, we will follow the writings of Stephen J. Rossetti, "Post-Crisis Morale Among Priests," *America* 191 (2004): 8–10 and "From Anger to Gratitude: Becoming a Eucharistic People," *Origins* 33 (2004): 757–762.

7. See also National Federation of Priests' Councils, *Evolving Vision of the Priesthood* (Collegeville, Minn.: Liturgical Press, 2003).

8. These surveys also show that many priests believe that other priests are hurting and suffering low morale. Twenty-nine percent of priests feel that "people now look at [them] with suspicion." See also Dean R. Hoge, *Evolving Visions of the Priesthood: Changes from Vatican II to the Turn of the New Century* (Collegeville, Minn.: Liturgical Press, 2003).

9. Rossetti, "Post-Crisis Morale Among Priests," 10.

10. For a commentary on the nature of good and evil, see John Paul II, *Memory and Identity* (New York: Rizzoli, 2005).

11. Rossetti, "From Anger to Gratitude: Becoming a Eucharistic People," 758–759.

12. See Archbishop Sean O'Malley, "Pastoral Letter on Vocations," *Origins* 34 (2005): 555.

Appendix Three

1. This list of signs and cautions was adapted with permission from Praesidium, Inc. 2005.

Permissions

Every effort has been made to locate and secure permission for the inclusion of all copyrighted material in this book. If any such acknowledgments have been inadvertently omitted, the publisher would appreciate receiving full information so that proper credit may be given in future editions.

Scripture citations are taken from the *New Revised Standard Version of the Bible,* copyright 1989 by the Division of Christian Education of the National Council of the Churches of Christ in the USA. All rights reserved. Used with permission.

Excerpts from the English translation of the *Catechism of the Catholic Church* for the United States of America, copyright © 1994, United States Catholic Conference, Inc.—Libreria Editrice Vaticana; English translation of the *Catechism of the Catholic Church: Modifications from the Editio Typica,* copyright © 1997, United States Catholic Conference, Inc.—Libreria Editrice Vaticana. Used with permission.

Excerpts from *Reaching Out,* Henri Nouwen. Copyright © 1986. All rights reserved. Used with permission of Random House, New York.

Excerpts from *Rise, Let Us Be on Our Way,* Pope John Paul II. Copyright © 2004. All rights reserved. Used with permission of Time Warner Trade Publishing, New York.

Excerpts from *New Commentary on the Code of Cannon Law,* John P. Beal, James A. Coriden, Thomas J. Green. Copyright © 2000. All rights reserved. Used with permission of Paulist Press, Mahwah, New Jersey.

Excerpts from Rilke on *Love and Other Difficulties: Translations and Considerations* by Rainer Maria Rilke, translated by John J. L. Mood. Copyright © 1975 by W. W. Norton & Company, Inc. Used with permission of W. W. Norton & Company, Inc.

Excerpts from *Patores Dabo Vobis,* Pope John Paul II. Copyright © 1992. All rights reserved. Used with permission of Libreria Editrice Vaticana, Vatican City, Italy.

Excerpts from "Instruction Concerning the Criteria for the Discernment of Vocations with Regard to Persons with Homosexual Tendencies in View of their Admission to the Seminary and to Holy Orders," Congregation for Catholic Education. Copyright © 2005. All rights reserved. Used with permission of Libreria Editrice Vaticana, Vatican City, Italy.

Excerpts from *The Four Loves* by C.S. Lewis, copyright © 1960 by Helen Joy Lewis and renewed 1988 by Arthur Owen Barfield, reprinted by permission of Harcourt, Inc.

Excerpts from the *Intimate Connection* © 1988 James B. Nelson. Used by permission of Westminster John Knox Press.